RECONSTRUCTING
'A' LEVEL ENGLISH

Open University Press
English, Language, and Education series
General Editor: Anthony Adams
Lecturer in Education, University of Cambridge

This series is concerned with all aspects of language in education from the primary school to the tertiary sector. Its authors are experienced educators who examine both principles and practice of English subject teaching and language across the curriculum in the context of current educational and societal developments.

TITLES IN THIS SERIES

RECONSTRUCTING 'A' LEVEL ENGLISH

Patrick Scott

Open University Press
Milton Keynes · Philadelphia

Open University Press
12 Cofferidge Close
Stony Stratford
Milton Keynes MK11 1BY

and
1900 Frost Road, Suite 101
Bristol, PA 19007, USA

First Published 1989

British Library Cataloguing in Publication Data

Scott, Patrick, *1949–*
 Reconstructing "A" level English– (English, language
 and education series)
 1. England. Secondary schools. Curriculum subjects:
 English literature. G.C.E. (A level) examinations.
 Syllabuses
 I. Scott, Patrick, *1949–* II. series
 820'.76

 ISBN 0-335-09594-1

Library of Congress Cataloging-in-Publicaton Data

Scott, Patrick
 Reconstructing "A" level English/Patrick Scott.
  p.   cm.—(English, language, and education series)
 Bibliography: p.
 Includes index.
 1. English language—Study and teaching (Secondary)—Great
Britain. I. Title   II. Series.
 LB1631.S33 1989
 428.4071'241—dc20   89–3350 CIP
 ISBN 0-335-09594-1

Typeset by Rowland Phototypesetting Limited
Bury St Edmunds, Suffolk
Printed in Great Britain by Biddles Ltd.,
Guildford and King's Lynn

Contents

General editor's introduction

Patrick Scott, English Adviser for Cleveland, is probably best known to many readers of this book as a past Chair of the National Association for the Teaching of English. He has also had considerable experience as a teacher of sixth form English and as the Head of a Sixth Form Centre. His experience in teaching students aged 16–19 is, therefore, considerable, and (as this book makes clear) by no means limited to the conventional sixth form. However, that notion of 'the sixth' (in Dr Arnold's phrase, 'My top 30 boys, the eldest, the strongest and the cleverest'), and the Advanced Level examination which has accompanied it since 1952, has a remarkably enduring quality.

In 1938 the Spens Report on secondary education commented:

> the sixth form is indeed the most characteristic and most valuable feature in a grammar school in the training of the character and sense of responsibility and on its existence depends all that is best in the grammar school tradition.

The notion of the sixth form has, therefore, never been far removed from a particular set of values. It is significant that the Report of the Higginson Committee, which put forward the latest in the many former suggestions for broadening the basis of 16–19 education (with a good deal of support from the university sector), was turned down unceremoniously, as soon as it was published, by the government of the day.

It so happens that I belong to that generation of grammar school sixth form pupils that took the Advanced Level examination for the first time. At that juncture it represented a considerable advance on what had preceded it. Yet, in 1988, one can find some papers in the summer 'A' level examination which contain questions and syllabuses virtually identical with the ones that I studied in the early 1950s. Patrick Scott's detailed analysis of the language and ideology of examination papers in this book shows clearly how much more is at stake here than just the content of an English course. 'A' level has persisted for so long (and resisted innumerable attempts at change) precisely because it incorporates a culture – the culture associated with the twin concepts of the 'grammar school' and the 'sixth form'. For those committed to comprehensive education these two concepts create a considerable problem, filled as they still are with great prestige in the eyes of students, teachers and parents alike. The 'sixth' and 'A' level still represent a kind of Holy Grail for many engaged in education, and the young teacher has generally to fulfil an apprenticeship before he or she is initiated into the sacred portals.

Yet, as this book explores, this static tradition is by no means incapable of change by those who wish to reformulate its basis. Indeed, as the comprehensive school has developed, the clientele for education beyond the age of 16 (the so-called 'new sixth') has also both changed and expanded. Institutions, too, have changed, with the sixth form college, the tertiary college and the sixth form centre becoming increasingly common forms of organization. All the evidence from research points to the greater satisfaction experienced by the age range concerned in being treated in a collegiate manner and given more responsibility for their own learning.

The contrast between this and the earlier stages of schooling, with the shift from school pupil to tertiary student, has been helpfully expressed by Ronald King, the first Principal of Exeter College (a tertiary college), in his book *School and College* (1976), published by Routledge and Kegan Paul:

> The college as an association represents the organizational form in which the principles of voluntarism of attendance and consumerism of provision may be expressed. When students register they are entering into a contract to which they owe obligations, mainly in relation to fulfilling the requirements of the course, and from which they obtain certain rights in terms of access to college facilities. Pupils have no contract. They have obligations, which are expected to be expressed as loyalties, but few rights. Rights may be taken away from them, such as being able to dress as they choose, and later returned as privileges.

At the same time, new patterns of examinations have evolved to meet the needs of this new population of students. The Associated Examining Board's Communication Studies paper at Advanced Level was a pioneer in this field in 1979 and has been followed very closely by other new syllabuses in English Language by both the London and the Northern Examination Boards. Yet, for most teachers, it is still traditional 'A' level English Literature that remains at the heart of 'A' level. The National Association for the Teaching of English, especially through the work of Bill Greenwell at Exeter College, has done a good deal to make more widely known the range of 'alternative' syllabuses that are available but, even so, their take up has been somewhat limited.

One of the features of Patrick's book is its scholarly account of the development and possibilities of such alternatives to traditional 'A' level that exist even at the present time. As more students go into post-16 education from the background of GCSE it is likely that these alternatives, especially those that involve course work, will become much more common. Those who have successfully completed a good GCSE course are unlikely to find the traditional set book course followed by the 3-hour paper to their liking.

Yet good work can be done even within this context. In 1981, Ted Hopkin (also of Exeter College) and I published *Sixth Sense* (Blackie), in which we looked at the history of 16–19 English education and gave examples of good practice at the time. That book is now inevitably out of date, but I am pleased to be able to bring the story up to date with the publication of the present volume. What we did find, however, in the case studies that we presented, was the range of good work that could go on in very different departments and under different philosophies of English teaching, including the most traditional.

What has always been needed is much greater eclecticism than has previously existed. Now that we have established English as a single concept embracing Language, Literature and Communication at GCSE, we need to move in the same direction at 16–19 also. Personally, I have little doubt that the future of post-16 English lies in the direction of some form of modular course, which is one of the possibilities discussed by Patrick Scott in the present volume. It is to be hoped that such a course will also lead to a broadening of the curriculum for this age range. It seems remarkable that the move towards ABC (the 'Agreement to Broaden the Curriculum') goes back to as long ago as 1962, and yet, supported as it was by many influential Headteachers, it achieved practically nothing.

It may be that the decline in numbers in this age range will force schools (as well as further and higher education) to make more changes in the direction that is needed, so as to appeal to those who might be prepared to stay on beyond the school leaving age. The present volume, which seeks to provide both a historical and contemporary perspective on the best of current practice, points to where this may lead us. However, its major contribution probably lies in its discussion of what might be loosely called the sociology of the sixth. It shows clearly why this nineteenth-century institution, curiously out of touch with present-day realities, has proved so enduring; it also shows why change of a radical nature is necessary if we are to provide adequate education for this age range in the latter days of the present century.

In planning the book, we had some discussion over the title. I wanted the focus to be upon the reconstruction of English teaching in the 16–19 age range. Patrick was adamant that the audience he wanted to reach was that of the traditional sixth-form teacher as well. Patrick was right – there is much to share in the best of the older and the newer traditions coming together. Those of us, like the author and myelf, who were the products of the old system, have much to be thankful for but, if the 'sixth' is in any sense to survive, it will have to adapt to new circumstances. The present volume shows, in terms of the English curriculum, some of the ways in which this change may take place.

Anthony Adams

Acknowledgements

A book of this kind both prompts and defies the attempt to acknowledge those who have been influential in shaping the values and beliefs that are contained within it. It is neither possible nor profitable to put a name tag on everything that happens to you as a teacher. None the less, I feel the need to say thanks to Peter Womack, for the discussions we have had intermittently ever since we first taught together, and similarly to Kerry Jones. I would also like to thank the members of the Northern Working Party on 'A' level English Language, and especially George Keith. I am not always given to being as awkward as I was while the JMB syllabus was making its way through the relevant Schools Council committees. Thanks, also, to Oonagh Walker at St Mary's Sixth Form College in Middlesbrough for drawing to my attention the work by Peter Stockwell.

It would be sentimental to name all the students that I have learned from. I would, however, like to pay tribute to the JMB examiners who, despite being shackled by the constraints of the traditional 'A' level syllabus, were still able to spot talent even when it manifested itself in the most unconventional students – Viv Symons, Gaynor Chew, Dawn Williams, Alan Sheeran and others. As a dedication, however, I would like this book to be for Angel and Abigail.

The author and publisher are grateful to the following for permission to reproduce copyright material: The Associated Examining Board for the 'A' level Communication Studies syllabus and for examination questions taken from a number of different papers. The comments made on these questions are the sole responsibility of the author and have not been provided or approved by the Board. The University of London School Examinations Board for the 'A' level English Language Studies syllabus and for questions taken from the 'A' level English Language Studies examination papers. ULSEB accepts no responsibility for any opinions expressed by the author about those questions or the way in which they might be answered. The Joint Matriculation Board for the 'A' level English Language syllabus and for questions taken from a number of examination papers. Where commentaries have been provided by the author, they are not the responsibility of the Examination Board and may not necessarily constitute the only possible solution. Steve Bennison, Andrew Spicer and the Avon Association for the Teaching of English for their syllabus in 'A' level English (Cultural Studies). Further details are available from the 'A' Level Working Party, 16 Burlington Road, Redland, Bristol B56 6TL. Peter Stockwell for 'Tom's Last Voyage'. Zoe Fairbairns and Virago Press for the extract from *Benefits* © copyright © Zoe Fairbairns 1979, published by Virago Press 1979, 1988.

1 Introduction

Imagine how, in an education system different from this one, proposals to introduce a new sixth-form examination might be received.

Outrage at changes to exam system

Government proposals to change the examination system for 18-year-olds were widely criticized yesterday following the publication of a consultation document *Examinations at 18+: An 'Advanced' Level*. Plans were unveiled to limit Sixth-form pupils to the study of 3 subjects. In English, for example, candidates would be required to choose 7 'set books' which, as matter of policy, would exclude both literature in translation and American writers. If these proposals are accepted, assessment will be entirely by end-of-course exam, designed to test how much pupils can remember about the books they have read. The President of the recently formed National Federation of Home/School associations commented that 'Candidates might have no more than 45 minutes to write about a book that may have been studied intensively over 6 or 7 weeks.'

Teachers' organizations greeted the changes with scepticism. 'They simply won't work', said the Chair of the National Association for the Teaching of English. 'We live in a multicultural society and we must retain our traditional freedom to choose appropriate material for our pupils.' Singled out for the fiercest criticism were the proposals to scrap all work on film, television and drama, and to ignore the new technology on the grounds that computers 'have contributed little of distinction to the literary canon'. Parents' groups and employers are particularly disturbed by the way in which the new syllabuses make no reference to Oral Communication, recently introduced at GCSE level, and pay scant regard to the range of writing that might be expected of an 18-year-old school leaver. In future, it was claimed, a candidate might be able to achieve a grade 'A' pass without writing anything other than literary criticism.

The point, of course, is that if a group of teachers, examiners and academics were put together in a room and told they could not come out until they had devised an 18+ exam, they would be unlikely to invent 'A' level English Literature. And if they did, they would probably unleash a storm of protest. How can the curriculum at 18+ so wilfully ignore large areas of the subject? How can such a cursory system of assessment possibly be considered adequate?

It is with the first of these questions in particular that this opening chapter is concerned. Even before the advent of GCSE the lack of continuity between English pre- and post-16 had begun to seem freakish. The problem is now more acute than ever, and some explanation of how it has arisen is essential as a preliminary to any serious discussion about possible reform.

There are obvious points to be made. Most commentators would probably draw attention to the influence wielded by university departments of English, and the difficulties of establishing a consensus for change, in a system that, post-16, is probably as varied as it is possible to be. Broad generalities of this kind, however, only beg further questions. Any account of the way in which post-16 English has been constrained by the dead hand of higher education, for example, has some explaining to do. Arguably, the subject has altered more dramatically at degree level and beyond than it has in school sixth forms. Similar objections can be raised to the proposition that change is hard to effect because the system has become impossibly complex and diverse. The variety of provision for 11- to 16-year-olds was never raised as an objection to the introduction of GCSE and certainly did nothing to hinder the growth of support for the new exam among secondary teachers.

If the alibis that are most commonly provided in defence of 'A' level English seem fairly unconvincing, it's because they are excuses rather than explanations. They assume some kind of agreement about the need for change that has been frustrated only by the practical difficulties of making it happen. What they ignore is the existence of ideological differences so fundamental that they have frozen post-16 English in its current form, while, until recently, remaining largely undeclared.

One way of flushing these differences into the open is to find a new vantage point, and there can be little doubt that the familiar outline of 'A' level English starts to look dangerously eccentric when examined in the light of practice elsewhere. Consider, for example, what is happening in Australia, in an education system sufficiently close to our own for the comparison to be a particularly interesting one.

Even though there is no obligation for any of the States to conform or even communicate with each other, developments across the country as a whole have often had a great deal in common:

> In no other country with the probable exception of New Zealand, can one find such widespread assimilation, adaptation and implementation of progressive theory into systems-wide curriculum orthodoxy.

The judgement is made by Paul Nay-Brock (1987) in *Who's Doing What?*, a description of the Senior English Curriculum in Australian Schools, and is based on first-hand experience of developments in many of the Australian states as well as in Great Britain. He quotes from a curriculum survey published in 1979 in order to characterize the most significant features of what he describes as the 'new English' orthodoxy. It is a list that will be familiar to many English teachers in this country engaged in teaching GCSE:

> A concern with personal growth throughout language development; a more or less explicit reliance on models of language learning in early childhood; a view of language as a complex inter-relationship between the four language 'skills' or 'arts' of listening, speaking, reading and writing; the belief that language is learned in use; the encouragement of activities such as small group work, drama and role play to provide a diversity of contexts for language use; the encouragement of the use of themes or units of work which integrated language study and literature study; the use of the child's own experience as a resource; recognising and building on the language knowledge children bring with them to the classroom; an emphasis on personal and imaginative writing; an emphasis on the exploration of language through informal talk; a recognition of diversity and a variety in language; a move away from the traditional view of one 'correct' form of standard English; a recognition of the need to respect the child's own use of language; and a view of the teacher as a facilitator of learning.

This passage becomes much more striking when it is remembered that Paul Nay-Brock is not just talking about the junior secondary curriculum:

> It has taken longer for these kinds of features to become prominent in the senior English curricula in Australia and the degree to which they and other features of the 'new English' appear in such syllabuses varies from system to system. But many of these new features can now be found embedded in the Australian senior secondary English curriculum within richly diversified State and Territory contexts of curricular products and processes.

The contrast with this country could hardly be more marked. While it would be naive to imagine that practice in Australia is as consistently different from practice in Britain as this account might imply, the comparison makes it possible to identify either end of the ideological spectrum in the kind of crude way that can sometimes be helpful in coming to terms with complex issues:

By tradition	*By revision*
'English' entails	'English' might become
the study of	the study of
Literature	• a variety of media including film, TV, radio and theatre
	• a range of written forms including literature
	• a range of oral uses of the language
from a predominantly Anglocentric point of view	deriving from a variety of cultures
employing literary critical techniques	using a variety of kinds of critical enquiry and encouraging the development of personal competence

assessed by examinations	assessed by course work
in which control is retained by the assessor.	in which control is handed over, at least in part, to the student.

Those features of the subject listed in the left-hand column are embodied in 'A' level English Literature, whereas those in the right-hand column only force their way on to the post-16 curriculum by courtesy of 'A' level English Language and 'A' level Communication Studies, both of which receive more detailed treatment in later chapters.

Until recently, the tendency for 'A' level English Literature to resist change was not felt by most teachers to be a serious problem. While traditional versions of English sometimes showed remarkable powers of survival, there was never any question but that they would ultimately disappear. They certainly did not pose any kind of threat to the continued development of the subject. This view achieved its most confident expression in *Growth through English*, first published in 1967, in which John Dixon outlined a 'map' of the 'confusing claims and theories', with which it was possible to demonstrate which versions of the subject had been superseded, which retained some credibility, and which might point to a better future:

> Among the models or images of English that have been widely accepted in schools on both sides of the Atlantic, three were singled out. The first centred on *skills*; it fitted an era when initial literacy was the prime demand. The second stressed the *cultural heritage*, the need for a civilising and socially unifying content. The third (and current) model focuses on *personal growth*: on the need to re-examine the learning processes and the meaning to the individual of what he is doing in English lessons. Looking back over the history of our subject, we see the limitations in the earlier models and thus the need to reinterpret our conception of 'skills' and 'heritage'.

There is no mistaking John Dixon's conviction that he had history on his side. It is less easy now to subscribe to this uncomplicated belief in progress. The metaphors that spring to mind as a way of describing what is happening to 'English' are no longer, convincingly, about 'Growth' or 'New Directions', but rather about conflict and compromise (consider the press reception of the 'Kingman Report') and ownership ('whose English?').

The significance of this is considerable. The days when it might have been possible to excuse the inadequacies of 'A' level English with a reassurance that the syllabuses had not yet been reformed are long gone. And with them has gone the illusion that the curriculum could be ideologically neutral. Where differences might once have been seen as an inevitable and untroubling feature of the gradual move towards an enlightened consensus, they must now be viewed as evidence of a disturbing fragmentation.

A crisis in the subject

The passage below offers an account of the development of English in the 1920s and 1930s, and its subsequent effect on the school curriculum. For reasons that will become apparent, it is being kept temporarily anonymous. If it is unfamiliar to you, have a guess at the date of publication:

> Practical criticism came to be harmful when it began to be used, not as an instructive exercise, but as a method for academics in English departments at universities to write their books and make their careers. Merely to indicate that he had read a work with care could not serve to establish an academic's reputation: he found himself obliged to discover a new and individual interpretation of the text (however well known) which was his subject. The academic critic had to search for all sorts of features of his text which were not obvious to the ordinary reader – patterning of imagery; hidden overtones, ambiguities and word-play; symbolism, ironies and self-parody – in order to produce an entirely new reading which had eluded all the work's readers until then, and would have continued to do so, had it not been for the critic's unusual percipience.
>
> Bright undergraduates, trained by these academics, became English teachers at schools and started to instruct their pupils in the methods they had learnt. They did not – as they might usefully have done – treat practical criticism as a way of sharpening beginners' attention to form and detail in the reading of literature. Rather, every poem became a puzzle; the jargon of literary criticism the means to solve it.

It is a curious piece of writing. A first reading suggests some kind of journalism; the heavy-handed irony at the expense of academics, for example, and the sneering comments aimed at virtually everybody else, would seem to rule out anything more serious. This verdict is supported by a closer look at the way in which the argument is advanced. The writer clearly feels under no obligation to provide supporting evidence – assertion is sufficient proof. If it is a piece of journalism, however, it is difficult to imagine quite where it might have appeared.

The invitation to suggest a publication date may have set alarm bells ringing. The rather testy way in which the author dismisses one of the most powerful intellectual traditions in the history of Literary Studies suggests that he has misjudged its likely influence. Such a mistake could hardly have been made much later than the end of the 1930s, though the chronology in the passage suggests a slightly later date. Maybe it is one of those infamous attacks on F. R. Leavis that were out of touch before they were even published.

If that, or something like it, was what you thought, then you were wrong. The passage is taken from *English our English*, written by John Marenbon and published by the Centre for Policy Studies in 1987. It is reproduced here because John Marenbon is the Director of Studies in English at Trinity College, Cambridge, and because the Centre for Policy Studies – 'the brain-box of the new Conservatism'[1]* – is listened to in government circles.

The Centre for Policy Studies is not alone in peddling views of this kind, however. Indeed, with hindsight, it is possible to say that in the current political climate the publication of *English our English*, or something very much like it,

---

*Superscript numerals refer to numbered notes at the end of the book.

could have been predicted. It is simply one particularly vivid illustration of what happens if you start to apply to education the nationalist thinking of the new right. Consider, for example, this piece from *The Guardian* (26 October 1987):

Right call for restoration of classics in 'anti-British' attack on GCSE

The new GCSE exam for 16-year-olds in England and Wales is anti-British and anti-educational, and an alternative exam, more like the traditional 'O' level, should be allowed in schools which choose to opt out of local education authority control, a group of new right thinkers argue in a book published today.

The book comes as hopes among the Latin lobby that ancient languages were to become 'foundation subjects' in the new national curriculum planned by the Government were dashed by authoritative Whitehall sources.

The new right is campaigning for Latin and Greek to be treated as foundation subjects rather than modern languages, but the sources made it plain that the national curriculum, designed to take up to 80 or even 90 per cent of teaching, still left time for schools where Latin was thriving – and these were dwindling in number – to teach the subject.

The GCSE, according to Ms Joanna North, editor of the book, poses a threat to 'real education'.

She writes: 'In the name of an egalitarian programme emphasising practical skills, and a training for life in the adult world, the GCSE is deeply anti-educational. Much that was of value in the old system will be lost for ever.'

Ms North says so-called multicultural education is also profoundly counter-educational. 'The sensitive appreciation of British culture, and British ways of life, is what is likely to disappear from education if the philosophy of the GCSE is successfully implemented.

'At best, the insistence on a multicultural perspective will destroy that sensitivity of outlook, and tolerance, of other peoples which traditional education, when most successful, encouraged and nurtured. At worst, the new politicised curriculum will be profoundly antagonising, serving to accentuate, and magnify, that which divides us.

'The explicit commitment to multicultural education gives to proponents of "anti-racism" the permission to pursue their fanatical and in truth hate-filled policies of censorship and thought-control.'

The GCSE: An Examination. £6.50. The Claridge Press, 8 Victoria Square, London SW1.

The references to 'British culture' and 'British ways of life' echo Marenbon (1987), who writes elsewhere in his pamphlet that: 'without some knowledge of classical literature an Englishman will always be to some extent a stranger to his own culture'. Both versions of 'culture' are, of course, exclusive, so it comes as no surprise that they need to be defended against their 'enemies' (Marenbon). Although the language of 'The GCSE: an examination' may be more conciliatory, the message is the same: 'Other people' remain estranged from British or, more ominously, 'our' culture.

'English' is particularly vulnerable to this kind of assault because it is both a language and a nation. The one provides a way of constructing an identity for the other, and literature can be fashioned into a powerful weapon against the intruder. It is possible to get the measure of this kind of crude nationalism by drawing a comparison with John Dixon's (1967) original description in *Growth through English* of the idealism that inspired those who first saw 'English' as a way of preserving and passing on a 'cultural heritage':

> Great literature offers, in Arnold's phrase, a criticism of life: what better could the children be reading? Here was a content for English that all could respect . . . Through literature all that was best in national thought and feeling could be handed on to a generation that knew largely slums and economic depression.

Changed economic circumstances and the loss of Empire have given a more competitive and aggressive edge to contemporary definitions of what it means to be or to write English.

It is a point made by Seamus Heaney in *North*, where he writes about how:

> I tried to write about the sycamores
> And innovated a South Derry rhyme
> With hushed and lulled full chimes for pushed and pulled.
> Those hob-nailed boots from beyond the mountain
> Were walking, by God, all over the fine
> Lawns of elocution.

By the end of the poem, Heaney's patience has run out. He is less jaunty, less tolerant:

> Ulster was British, but with no rights on
> The English Lyric: all around us, though
> We hadn't named it, the ministry of fear.

What is at stake is not simply a curriculum (is it ever?) but an inheritance. It is no accident that the solutions in Australia, where there is less invested in the concept of 'Standard English' and where the relationship between the literary canon and a national culture is a more distant and problematic one, have been different ones. The 'crisis' in the subject stems from the realization that there can be competing versions of Literature, and that the differences matter.

It is arguable, however, that the groundwork for this kind of ideologically inspired assault on the curriculum was laid long before the new right had become a force to be reckoned with. If attempts are now being made to annex English Literature for Queen and country, it is because the theorists had already drawn attention to the ideological presumptions of the old consensus. The best way of illustrating this point is to consider what has happened to English in higher education over the last two decades.

The first and most important point to make is that it is no longer possible to be an innocent reader. Literary theory has put paid to that convenient camouflage by insisting that critics are implicated in any interpretation that they might offer. It has also inflicted some damage on that other, always less convincing, myth of the innocent writer. The author is no longer the towering genius, but historically and socially specific. In *Marxism and Literature*, Raymond Williams (1977) puts it like this:

> as a social individual he [the writer] is [also] specific, but within the social forms of his time and place. The crucial argument, then, turns on the nature of that specificity and these forms, and on the relations between them. In the case of the writer one of these social forms is central: his language.

By insisting that both production and interpretation are relative, literary theory invites the reader to be much more 'playful' than in the past. No longer is it necessary for versions of a text to be in competition with each other; they can co-exist, or even, on occasion, be mutually illuminating. That opens a number of doors. It is only possible, after all, to understand what writers and readers bring to texts by enlisting the aid of the social sciences. At its most conventional, this means history. But equally important have been the insights culled from linguistics, psychology, anthropology and sociology, as well as from a variety of disciplines that are subsumed by these – biography, women's studies, semiotics, and so on. Reading has become less a quest for the Holy Grail, more a matter of charting the route.

Where the new criticism demanded an exclusive focus on the text – 'the words on the page' – literary theory actively encourages the reader to explore the wider context within which the text exists and without which its meaning is only imperfectly understood. That wider context might include, for example, study of the deep narrative structures on which it draws, the economic circumstances of its production, or contemporary assumptions about social mores.

The ideologies of the new right needed no second invitation. The 'subject' was so busy deconstructing itself that the theorists were actively dismissive of any opinion that was not explicit about its own ideology. There could hardly be a better opportunity for challenging the liberal humanist consensus, or for questioning how it was manifested in schools.

A crisis in the institutions

In an unpublished paper, *Changing 'A' levels*, delivered to the 1987 Higher Education Teachers of English (HETE) conference, Peter Womack, a lecturer in English at the University of East Anglia, establishes some important links between the particular 'crisis' in the subject and the more general loss of confidence in the institutions whereby it is embodied. Citing Foucault, he starts by identifying the type of discourse commonly employed in writing about literature:

> the essay – that is a type of writing which, by evading the specifications of function on the one hand and those of artistic form on the other, just about managed to pass itself off as writing in general – the direct embodiment of thought.

This, he argues, is the characteristic voice of the intellectual – detached, omniscient, Olympian.

Contrasted with this are, in Foucault's words, 'those intellectuals who were merely *competent instances* in the service of the state or capital – technicians, magistrates, teachers'. Their role, and their language, is recognizable by its preoccupation with function, by its humdrum concern with achieving things rather than contemplating them. Peter Womack (1987) continues:

> Foucault's argument, crudely summarised, is that . . . intellectuals 'have become used to working, not in the modality of the "universal", the "exemplary", the "just-and-true-for-all", but within specific sectors, at the precise points where their own conditions of life or work situate them (housing, the hospital, the asylum, the laboratory, the university, family and sexual relations).' This process of specification is surely what is being reflected, or rather produced and contested in education. The universal truths whose integrity made possible the disciplinary boundaries and didactic methods of the grammar school curriculum no longer command a histori- cally possible subject for their utterance. The result is a multiple revaluation: a questioning of the privileged educational role of writing itself; an identity crisis in the *general* institution (the comprehensive school); a growth, among educationalists, politicians, and most importantly, kids, of an instrumental view of education in general and English in particular; and in the study of literature, a pervasive textual libertarianism, a feeling that the question of the *truth* of a student's observations on a text is not as important as we used to think, partly because the criteria of such truth have little authority, and partly because, in any case, the educative value of the whole business lies in the process by which the observations are formulated, and not in the end-product.

This is not an easy argument, but it is an important one. The essential distinction is between 'universal truths' and the 'process of specification'. On the one hand, there is an intellectual tradition which seeks to embody 'truth' in a set of secure generalizations. On the other, there is a world which, ever more successfully, resists any such impulse. In place of the grand design, there is now only the more modest ambition to illuminate the process of intellectual enquiry.

If Peter Womack is right, then 'A' level English Literature in its present form has nothing to look forward to but a long, lingering decline. Except as a kind of junior version of the real thing, it will become increasingly difficult to sustain a subject that deliberately averts its gaze when confronted with its own reflection.

By this version of events, nostalgia about the 'cultural heritage' is merely a side-show, not the main performance. More powerful forces are at work, forces that make traditional claims for the subject seem increasingly difficult to maintain, and the school curriculum a more hostile environment. Consider, for example, Denys Thompson in 1965:[2]

> The case for literature is that it stands for humanity at a time when human values are not upheld . . . among these values we number imagination, as well as the obviously acceptable ones like sympathy, understanding and tolerance.

When he made this point, Denys Thompson was speaking to a conference of the National Council for the Teaching of English (USA), and his brief was to provide an international perspective on the state of the art. It is difficult, now, to imagine a world in which this was thought to be convincing. It no longer suggests a way in which the subject might be taught, or students encouraged to opt for it. No ambitious head of department could realistically use it to support a bid for additional resources, and it seems alarmingly flimsy as the starting point for framing a school policy. The conceptual shift identified by Foucault has moved apace, leaving some grand ideals in its wake.

The institutions have geared themselves up to a very different set of imperatives. In 1965, curriculum debate was about what happened to children that passed the 11+. As Peter Womack points out, English Literature was secure within the 'disciplinary boundaries and the didactic method of the Grammar school curriculum'. The comprehensive school posed a new set of problems because it reopened debate about the purposes of education. When children of all kinds are educated together, questions about how or whether to differentiate between them cannot be avoided. And 'universal truths' are unlikely to prove the most appropriate tools with which to set about devising a curriculum for the comprehensive school. The new system both reflected and promoted the general tendency towards 'specification', with all the fragmentation that that term implies.

In post-16 education, these changes were experienced in a wholly distinctive way. The voluntary nature of the sector allowed schools and colleges to respond not by devising a curriculum, but by licensing a marketplace. What was offered to potential students were the courses judged likely to attract most takers. In the absence of any alternative ideas, consumer demand became the guiding principle. It was a far cry from the high-minded ideals of the grammar school.

It is also worth recalling that there was another logic at work reinforcing further the tendency towards being 'open access' and free market. Just as the natural outcome of selection is to discard children in ever increasing numbers as they move through the system, so the natural inclination of a comprehensive system is to recruit them. Where one seeks to exclude, the other attempts to retain.

The effect of all this on the post-16 curriculum was complex and subtle. It can most easily be traced, however, by looking at the way in which teachers' expectations are altered by the context within which they work. Because a selective system is predicated upon the notion of a limited reservoir of talent, there is always a ready explanation for failure; if they do not meet the grade, they are not suited to an academic education. The fault lies not in ourselves, but in our stars. There is no need for teachers to reproach either themselves or the institutions in which they work.

For teachers from schools or colleges who are sympathetic towards the logic of the comprehensive system, the opposite is the case. Those of their students who fail 'A' level are not just unfortunate casualties. As well as failing, they have been failed. Their potential has not been realized. They are evidence that the system needs reform.

From this impulse began a series of initiatives for syllabus reform that were, and continue to be, quite ambivalent about whether it is the student, the subject or the method of assessment that is at fault. By resigning themselves to the continuation of 'A' level as a 'standard', the reformers had set themselves a daunting task. It is hard to create an alternative syllabus that both departs from and is comparable with what it is intended to replace.

Despite this, new 'A' level syllabuses continued to be published throughout the 1970s and 1980s with increasing regularity. The enthusiasm for reform was happily matched by further institutional changes that made it possible for innovation to be reassuringly piecemeal. Small sixth forms capable of raising only one or two 'A' level groups in a year had been constrained by the understandable tendency to treat as a kind of veto the wishes of students with conventional literary aspirations. Sixth Form and Tertiary Colleges, with anything up to 10 or more groups in a year, had no such inhibitions. 'Communication', 'English Language', alternative syllabuses of all kinds, could be introduced for anybody who wished to opt for them. The customer was always right.

While this may have been tactically expedient, it led, of course, to a further fragmentation of the 'English' curriculum. It is interesting to speculate about what might have happened if the institutional pressures had worked in the opposite direction, and forced all change to be incorporated within a single syllabus. Ironically, the outcome of a decade of experimentation has been a confirmation of the ascendancy of English Literature.

Proposals for reform

Despite everything, however, 'A' level has flourished, and the number of centres offering 'alternative' syllabuses remains small, which suggests that this chapter might have been applying itself to the wrong question. Perhaps less attention should have been paid to the alleged weaknesses of 'A' level and more to its evident strengths. Why should an exam which turns the English curriculum pre-16 on its head, and persists as a model of bad practice in assessment, be so resilient?

In one sense, 'A' level is successful not because it offers what people want or because it embodies profound curriculum thinking but because it is there. It provides the currency of post-16 education, and like most forms of currency it can readily adapt itself to new circumstances. Despite starting life as the standard for an authoritarian grammar school curriculum, it has experienced few difficulties in adjusting to the marketplace of open access education post-16.

A complete answer to the question about why 'A' level has endured, however, has to go further than this. It has to provide an explanation of why the several attempts at structural reform have also come to grief. Most well-known of these were the proposals for 'Q' and 'F' ('Qualifying' and 'Final') advanced in 1969, and the more recent 'N' and 'F' ('Normal' and 'Further') which were published in 1978. Both of these proposals stemmed from a set of principles established by the Schools Council and the Standing Conference on University Education (SCUE) in 1966, which can be summarized as follows:[3]

1 The number and academic range of sixth form students were increasing,
2 It was desirable to broaden the scope of study and to reduce specialisation,
3 It was desirable to allow pupils to make their choice of career as late as possible, which early narrowing of the curriculum impeded.

At first glance, this looks like a forward-looking programme based upon realistic and dispassionate judgements about the future. The received wisdom about why it was never realized is that the Schools Council allowed the broad aims, which had attracted some support, to become obscured by the practical details of each succeeding scheme. It was also widely held that the Council had underestimated how resistant schools would be to change of any kind, whatever its provenance.

Although there may be an element of truth in this view, it does not explain why the lack of enthusiasm for N and F was so universal. The advocates of reform might reasonably have expected some support. In the event, it was almost non-existent. This reluctance to stand up and be counted suggests that the problem lay not with the specific proposals but with the principles that informed them, the very principles that had attracted so much apparent support.

Re-examined in the light of what has happened since, those three principles look less like a programme for the future, and more like the last gasp of a system that was already on the way out. Recalling Foucault, it is possible to see the two principles at the heart of it all, about broadening the curriculum and delaying career choice, as a vain attempt to adapt the grammar school curriculum to a new set of circumstances. Both derive from a liberal humanist view of the nature of knowledge and the purposes of education. Broadening the curriculum was not seen as a way of dismantling subjects but of introducing students to more of them. And if career choices were delayed until the last possible minute, it would be easier to ignore the vocational needs of students and develop the subject-based curriculum according to conventional notions about the nature of intellectual enquiry – as the pursuit of the universal.

Though the arguments were not articulated in this way, it is possible to detect in the more practical objections that were raised some feeling that the Schools Council principles were the solution to a different and less pressing problem. It was difficult, for example, to imagine how an extension on the *existing* curriculum – greater 'breadth' – was going to meet the needs of a group of 16- to 19-year-olds whose main distinguishing feature was that they were '*new*' sixth formers.

Since nobody was likely to campaign on the proposition that the 16–19 curriculum should be narrow, 'breadth' became a virtue by default. But it demanded an almost wilful disregard of practicalities. The most important of these was apparent from even a cursory acquaintance with developments in higher education. With a serene disregard for what was being proposed for the education of 16–19 year olds, the traditional academic disciplines were continuing to splinter and multiply. In an intellectual climate of this kind, it was almost impossible to see any way of reversing the tendency towards specialization without creating intolerable pressures. English exemplifies this point precisely. The 'subject' has expanded to include Linguistics, Communications, Media Education, and so on, all possible courses of study at University or Polytechnic. The unanswered question was about how they could all be contained within the reduced time available for 'English' in a broad curriculum.

Perhaps more of a problem than this, however, is that the price to be paid for having a curriculum that maintains subject boundaries while also offering greater breadth is syllabuses that are more superficial. And it is almost impossible to imagine any kind of reform in which examinations at 18+ are made less academically demanding. Indeed, it is arguable that, since the introduction of 'A' level in 1951, syllabuses have become increasingly tough, particularly in the science subjects. Advanced Supplementary (AS) levels provide a vivid illustration of this universal tendency. The only politically acceptable version of an intermediate examination turns out to be one based on the ludicrous principle that 'standards' can remain comparable with 'A' level, when students are being expected to follow twice as many subjects in half the amount of time.

It is hardly surprising that the N and F proposals foundered. Their downfall was not that they were too radical, but that they were too cautious. They did nothing to alter the existing relationship between users and providers. The system by which academic qualifications provided the main route into work, and the curriculum from the age of 14 was dominated by the need to identify 19-year-olds who could be admitted to higher education, remained essentially intact. What N and F amounted to was a partial rationalization, and if it was envisaged that the system should remain unchanged, it was difficult to see why schools should be persuaded to swap one kind of compromise for another.

In the time since N and F was abandoned, the tensions in the system have become more acute, but little of real importance has changed. It is difficult to predict how much longer the status quo can be maintained. GCSE clearly puts 16–19 education under further pressure by creating a kind of student whose previous experience has been much more child-centred than in the past, who feels at ease with a wide variety of media and forms (of which literature is but one), and who is used to a pedagogy that blurs the distinction between 'doing' and 'reflecting'. No doubt, it will be quite possible to integrate 16-year-olds such as these into highly conventional 'A' level courses, but at the expense of continuity and not without causing problems for some that will only be resolved by dropping out.

The succeeding chapters, then, will look in more detail at the precise nature of what those problems are likely to be, both in conventional English Literature syllabuses and in the more novel alternatives. It may be helpful to make explicit the questions about English that are being addressed throughout, so that the particular instance can easily be related to the general point.

- What are the characteristics of the version of English Literature that is most widely promoted in school and college sixth forms?
- Can this version of English Literature be easily distinguished from the variety of 'alternative' syllabuses that have flourished during the last 10 years?
- What is the nature of the challenge that has been mounted by other, related 'subjects' ('English Language', 'Communications')?
- What forms of study are likely to be needed in order to ensure the survival of English as a significant part of the curriculum post-16? What position will be accorded to the study of literature?

2 Literature I: custom . . .

The picture roughly sketched in the introduction is one of a subject collapsing under the strain of too many irreconcilable ideologies and expectations. While GCSE may have sorted out the problems of what should be examined at 16, 'A' level remains vulnerable to the individual whims of teachers, examiners, academics and politicians. It is, to speak plainly, a muddle, and the closer you get to it the more of a muddle it appears to be.

'A disconcerting range of methods and expectations'

The recent HMI report[1] on the teaching of 'A' level English Literature provides a convenient place to start, pinpointing as it does the lack of any consensus about what the subject is or how it should be taught:

> Many schools did not have a coherence in their work and there was often a disconcerting range of methods and expectations of the students.

Though it is done with some delicacy, the Inspectorate do not leave much room for doubt about where the blame lies: 'there was the tacit assumption in departments that teachers were working with common and agreed aims which did not need specific discussion'. And the report goes on to reflect about some of the areas in which policy might be made more explicit:

- The kinds of reading and writing required to produce fluent and independent students.
- Progression through the course, and the implications of students' 'maturing perceptions'.
- Sequence of set book study.
- Appeal and suitability of set books.
- The place of critical course material.
- Range of reading.

As with most HMI reports the recommendations seem irreproachable. The report accurately reflects what most 'A' level teachers would acknowledge to be the case, in a way that sharpens our perception of the problem and provides clear guidance about what might be done to solve it. Few teachers would wish seriously to take issue with the proposition that 'A' level courses should have sorted out some answers to the questions asked by the Inspectorate.

Somehow, though, it is not as simple as that. The report leaves the unmistakable impression that the only obstacles to progress are the constraints of time, resources and accommodation. Formidable difficulties indeed, but capable of being overcome if reasonable people can just get together and agree on what they need to do. The world of this report is one in which teachers who lecture their students do so only because they have not yet appreciated how inefficient 'teacher monologue' is as a way of developing student response. There is nothing to hint that some teachers may choose to lecture because they believe that the student's individual response is fallible and untrustworthy and can only be properly trained by regular contact with a widely experienced and well-informed reader such as themselves. And there is nothing to indicate what a beleaguered head of department might do about it.

More surprising is the lack of any sustained comment about the role of the examination boards. When they do get a mention, it is to refute the allegation that they are responsible for bad practice. What needs correction are not the exams, but the teachers' perception of them. Reference is made both to what the boards 'were *believed* to want' and to 'what were *perceived* to be the requirements of successful writing for examination purposes'. The report does not explain why teachers who, elsewhere, are described as 'well matched to the courses in terms of academic qualifications and experience' should behave like rabbits caught in the headlights of an oncoming car when confronted with an examination and so mistake its actual demands that, for no good reason, they destroy any appreciation and enjoyment of the literature about which they are both 'erudite' and 'enthusiastic'.

What the report does not do, in other words, is to recognize what might happen if all those teachers who get along reasonably well with each other so long as policy remains 'tacit' were actually to follow the Inspectorate's advice and try to reach agreement. In this sense the report is innocent of ideology, though its authors are, no doubt, well aware of how deep the divisions lie. Indeed, it is not unreasonable to speculate that in some departments steps are being taken actively to avoid the kind of discussion that is being proposed by HMI.

While a department can avoid damaging ideological trench warfare by refusing to open hostilities, underlying differences will inevitably surface in the daily business of managing the work. Imagine, for example, a departmental meeting of 'A' level teachers called to standardize the marking for an internal examination. The opportunities that this provides for sniper fire are legion. A couple of examples might help to illustrate what kind of principles are at stake, and why they matter.

Imagine how two different candidates might respond to the following essay title:

Define and illustrate the different comic effects Jonson creates in Volpone.[2]

For one candidate this is clearly an opportunity to reproduce *as a list* all the types of comedy they have unearthed in *Volpone*. Their preparation for the examination will almost certainly have been concerned to categorize and file away literary effects to be retrieved when the time comes.

The second candidate, of a different frame of mind or taught by a different teacher, might well choose a different way of responding. For them, the word 'define' offers an opportunity to investigate first principles, to try to identify the springs of comedy in the play. That demands an essay that is more sequential, one which traces a developing argument. Placed beside the first answer, it would look quite different, presenting the teachers with a tricky problem of establishing common criteria for assessment.

A familiar enough dilemma, it might be thought, and one which simply demands the exercise of professional judgements. A fair point, but the choice between these two approaches is not a neutral one. It is not simply a matter of deciding which student is most skilful. The decisions made about the structure of the essay reflect a whole network of beliefs about the nature of critical commentary, what it is for, and what it can achieve, and hard as they may try to pretend that what a student writes in an examination is their own unaided work, all the teachers at this hypothetical department meeting know that what their students write will reflect what has been taught.

In structuring the essay as a list, the first student is demonstrating what he *knows* about the book: the matter, the content of the work, is being rehearsed as information, as fact. In choosing to construct the essay as an argument, the second student is acknowledging that the matter is contentious, and that the reader (of the essay) needs to be persuaded. She is demonstrating what she *thinks* about the book. Discussion about standards cannot but reflect the extent to which teachers value one or other of these two approaches, and provide fertile ground for quite serious controversy.

If the structure of an essay can cause difficulties, then what the students actually say is even more problematic. Take, for example, *Measure for Measure*. The question is about the Duke:

The Duke is not a Godlike figure, or a benign presence, but an unsympathetic and deceiving bungler. Do you agree?

This time, the two candidates may both have chosen to construct their answers in a similar way, but have come to radically different conclusions. One argues that, in conventional Shakespearean fashion, the Duke's intervention at the end of the play ensures that justice is done. Order is restored to the state, and harmony to individual relations as represented by the forthcoming marriage of the Duke and Isabella. It is an interpretation that relies heavily on a particular perception of how

Shakespeare responds to the dramatic conventions of the theatre within which he was working. Intolerant of ambiguity, it expects to find, in a successful work of art, unity and resolution.

The second candidate finds in the play something else entirely. In her version, the final scene is grotesque, parodic. The Duke, having admitted his own shortcomings in scene 1, returns merely because his attempts to meddle in the lives of others are about to fall dangerously apart. His proposal to Isabella and her silence provide an ironic contrast with Angelo who at least recognizes that his advances may be unwelcome. The Duke's 'justice', and his mercy, in the final act is as corrupt as it has always been. According to this view of the play, Shakespeare turns the dramatic conventions of the time to satiric purpose. Order and reconciliation are no more than grim jokes. It is a view of the play which accepts that the issues may be left unresolved, and that a work of art may make reference outside itself, to be not a unity, but a commentary, a reflection on the world rather than an abstraction from it.

In so far as any system of assessment at 'A' level must acknowledge the possibility of different, even opposing, interpretations, no distinctions should be drawn between these two candidates merely on the basis of which point of view they have chosen to adopt. In practice, once again, it is not quite so simple. Imagine how an examiner might feel about the shortcomings of the reading provided by the first student. Put bluntly, the candidate is not sophisticated enough to be able to sense Shakespeare's satiric intention which, after all, is only yielded by a most sensitive reading of the text. To compound the error, he has failed to account for Isabella's silence, a clear pointer to Shakespeare's intentions. Work of this quality simply does not deserve a higher mark. If, on the other hand, you prefer to direct your criticisms at the second candidate, you might wish to argue that she has not done her homework, since she is clearly unaware of the conventional symbolic force attached by Shakespeare to marriage. A weakness of this kind must be reflected in the marks that are awarded.

Both of these imaginary judgements on hypothetical essays are based on criteria commonly employed to assess essays for 'A' level English Literature, yet both discriminate on the basis of interpretation. And it is no solution to ignore the opinions that have been expressed. Why teach literature if you are unwilling to make distinctions between one response and another? The truth of the matter is that the quality of the response and the nature of the interpretation are not divisible in any easy way. The disagreement about whether an essay should be graded B, say, or E, can just as often be traced back to ideology as to any more 'professional' concerns.

Inconsistencies and confusions

It has been convenient to represent the differences between ideologies as differences between individuals. In practice, of course, it does not happen in quite such a neat and manageable way. The challenge for the student is not one of deciding between two distinct points of view, but of constructing a coherent view of what the subject is about in the first place.

By looking at examiners' reports, it is possible to piece together a picture of what students who have reached the end of an 'A' level course in English Literature actually think they have been doing for the previous 2 years. The examiners' complaints convey a vivid impression of what many sixth formers understand by 'literature' and by 'criticism'.

In their 1986 report, the AEB examiners conveniently summarize some of the major issues in the form of 'topics for class discussion':

> How far should art be seen as reality? Is it a good idea to speculate on what would have happened if the characters had not done what they did?
>
> Does it matter if when quoting poetry you make it look like prose and, if so, why?
>
> Which gives more literary satisfaction: simplification of the complex or continued pursuit of the elusive?

While there is a hint of exasperation in the way that these questions are phrased, they are genuinely representative of what examiners feel about the way in which 'A' level candidates view literature. Consider, for example, the similarities between the first two questions posed by the AEB examiners and these observations made in the JMB report from the same year (1986):

> A more sophisticated sense of the complex relationship between literary 'reality' and life itself was often required; too frequently the sole criterion was 'could we meet this character in real life?' (in response to a question on Dickens)

And, in a general comment on the set books paper: 'Some candidates . . . treated poetry as if it were a tiresome form of prose.'

What emerges from putting the two reports beside each other in this way is that different candidates entered for different syllabuses offered by different exam boards make strikingly similar mistakes. In one sense, this may seem a quite unremarkable point, hardly worth making, but it does suggest some interesting lines of thought. Two possible explanations occur. Either, for developmental reasons, a great many 18-year-olds are unable to cope with the demands made of them by literature, or there is a common heritage of teaching about literature which is actively disabling. It is beyond the scope of this book to disentangle the two in any definitive way, but there are points to be made about examination questions, for example, which suggest that the time honoured traditions of 'A' level teaching must bear some of the blame.

First, though, it is worth putting some more flesh on the bones of those typical students of 'A' level Literature who are busy driving their examiners to distraction. It is unlikely that many such students have given a great deal of conscious thought to any of the questions posed by the AEB. If asked, for example, about the nature of the relationship between literature and life, their instinctive response would probably be that what happens in books or on the stage mimics reality. That much they would feel to be obvious, until their attention was drawn to specific instances of books that clearly contradict this straightforward view. Having adjusted their opinions accordingly, they would still find it hard to accept the implications of what they had acknowledged. They would probably continue, for example, to judge episodes in novels by how 'realistic' they appear to be, and to respond to characters without reference to the context in which they are presented.

The problem, of course, is to do with how well they understand the category of 'literature', and while the examiner's reports specifically draw attention to the difficulties that students experience with poetry, the general point is true of other literary forms. Sixth-form students tend to find form or genre invisible. They simply fail to perceive its existence because they take it as axiomatic that literature is about something ('the theme'), and that their job as critics is to unearth what that is. While the JMB report makes this point several times, it is the examiner for paper III – unseen criticism – who puts it most interestingly: 'It was very noticeable', he comments, 'that many simply did not know what to do with a poem that had no "message" or "moral".'

One solution to this, commonly adopted by students that appreciate the point but find it difficult to respond appropriately, is described by the JMB:

> Many candidates appear to come armed with a stylistic 'hit list', devoting disproportionate time and energy to the location of such features as onomatopoeia, assonance, alliteration, rhyme, rhythm, metre and stanza form etc. even when they are not there.

Given that the whole process of writing and reading literature must seem fairly bewildering to anybody who approaches it in this way, it is hardly surprising that when students are asked to state a preference, they opt for the simple rather than the complex, for literature that is unambiguously plain, rather than richly layered. There is something disingenuous about the way in which, in their third 'topic for class discussion', the AEB examiners regret the failure to tackle what is complex and elusive. For many 'A' level students it must all seem equally impenetrable.

Because this account has relied upon the testimony of the examiners, it has tended to minimize the responsibility that they must accept for some of the difficulties they describe. The messages that are being conveyed, both explicitly in their reports and implicitly in their question papers, are by no means as clear as they might be. The following two questions, both taken from the same examination paper, are particularly interesting in the light of the examiners' concern about the representation of reality in literary texts:

> Jonson's characters in Volpone lack credibility. Is this a fair criticism?[3]

> Discuss the comment that, as human beings, the characters in Waiting For Godot do not interest us.[4]

While conceding that the underlying assumptions made in these questions about how the two plays should be approached are very different, it is not difficult to see that they both hinge upon the knotty problem of what criteria should be employed in judging the success of a work of literature. And both questions are ambiguous.

In the first example the criterion for answering the question is provided in the quotation – 'credibility'. Only by a cunning misreading of the question that follows could the candidate challenge the assumption that this is a useful way of talking about Ben Jonson's dramatic technique. The terms of the debate are given.

It is difficult, however, to know quite what those terms are. What does 'credibility' actually mean? A convincing case could be made for a variety of different interpretations. The most obvious seizes on the evident sense of 'credible' as 'believable' and naturally takes believable to mean realistic. After all, no suggestion is provided of any other yardstick by which to make such a judgement than 'life'. Does it convince you that events of this kind might actually have happened?

It takes a more sophisticated mind to interpret 'credible' as consistent or coherent. In other words, to provide a criterion for judging credibility that refers not outwards to 'reality' but inwards to the play itself. It would take some confidence to sustain this view, since there is nothing in the question to confirm whether it is justified or not. If this is what the question is asking, then, again, no attempt is made to ask whether it is any more satisfactory a way of describing Ben Jonson's work than to ask whether it is realistic.

Other interpretations are more difficult to sustain, but 'A' level candidates are often driven to desperate measures. It could quite justifiably be understood, for example, as a question not about literary technique but about morality. A question that asks not whether the characters are true to life, but whether they embody a higher truth.

Pity the poor student forced to select between these alternatives, uneasily aware that examiners are constantly berating them for not 'answering the question exactly'.[5] Is it surprising that many take the safest route and discuss Jonson's characters as we might 'meet (them) in real life'.

The question about *Waiting For Godot* that was linked with this offers a similar set of problems. Obviously, the key phrase is 'as human beings'. The form of words in which the question is cast – 'Discuss the comment that . . .' – seems to allow the candidates greater freedom to question the critical assumptions that are being made by, as it were, putting everything up for grabs. The phrasing of the rest of the question, however, leaves room to doubt this. If more weight is intended to be attached to the phrase 'as human beings' than the syntax would actually suggest, then it is either a very silly or a very sophisticated question to ask 'A' level candidates. Very silly because it is patently stupid to talk about *Waiting for Godot* as if it was in any sense a direct representation of reality, very sophisticated because it is surely asking a lot of most 18-year-olds to engage in explicit debate about why it is silly.

Both of these illustrations leave open the question of whether the examiners are themselves in a muddle about the way in which reality is represented in literature, whether they habitually overestimate the intellectual maturity of 18-year-olds or whether the questions are just poorly expressed.

Other examples suggest, however, that, particularly when they are trying to provide questions that students will feel confident about, the examiners often encourage the vices that they subsequently deplore in their reports. This is the AEB again:

> Her adventures are criminal, but she herself is not the criminal type. Discuss this view of Moll in Defoe's novel.[6]

The addition of those three words in the quote 'the criminal type' alter the question significantly. By introducing a terminology that smacks of popular psychology, questions are begged about what Defoe is doing in the novel. Arguably, his concern is not with Moll Flanders as a personality at all, any more than he is interested in the psychology of Crusoe. His novels are indeed realistic in that, through attention to detail, they create a powerful sense of a substantial material world. But it is a mistake to think that, for this reason, the characters embody some kind of psychological truth. The realism serves a different kind of purpose. It is so vividly realized because Defoe's concern is with property, with an economic rather than psychological reality.

It might be argued that candidates are free to challenge the question in exactly these terms, but if they are, then it is not made clear. On the contrary, the instruction specifically asks the candidate to focus on the character, not the book. It seems unaware that points might need to be made about the novel form.

The JMB examiners fall into the same trap, and they do so for similar reasons:

> We lose sympathy with Hamlet: his self-questioning is morbid and he makes feeble excuses for delaying his revenge. How far do you agree?[7]

The colloquial tone of 'feeble' and, arguably, 'morbid' suggests an attempt to talk to students in a language they can understand. In this aim, the question was most probably successful. The reason for citing it here, however, is that while, on the surface at least, it does not ask candidates to stray beyond the text, it does encourage them to read the play in the same way that, famously, Leavis accused Bradley of reading *Othello*. It is not, wrote Leavis, 'a psychological novel written in dramatic form and draped in poetry'.[8]

The cause of much of this confusion is the kind of critical language that is commonly employed in 'A' level teaching. The particular circumstances under which literature is studied and examined in schools have encouraged the growth of a specialized critical vocabulary which is now so familiar that, far from being identified as the cause of many of the difficulties that students experience in reading, it is viewed as the remedy. It is a balm that actually irritates the condition.

This critical terminology finds its most public expression in study aids. They are worth a brief look because they are undeniably influential and because they almost certainly reflect, as well as reinforce, critical approaches that are widely adopted in schools. It might be objected that 'A' level work is conducted at a significantly more sophisticated level than most study guides ever manage to reach. If this is the case, a lot of students seem unaware of it. The study guides provide some of the biggest profits in educational publishing.

They are of interest here, then, not so much for the quality of their critical observations, but for the way in which they process a literary text. The chapter headings tell their own story, and, whatever series you choose to look at, the pattern is remarkably similar.

The author and his work	Historical Background
The Elizabethan Theatre	Sean O'Casey's Life
The text of Shakespeare's plays	The works of Sean O'Casey
Synopsis, source and treatment of plot	The structure of Juno and the Paycock
Theme, atmosphere and setting	Characterisation
Structure and Style	Themes
Characters	Style
Act summaries, textual notes and revision questions	Notes on the text
General Questions	Questions on the play
(Brodie's *King Lear*)	(Methuen's *Juno and the Paycock*)

These chapter headings simply follow popular conventions about how a book can be reduced to manageable proportions, so that critical commentary falls into a series of watertight compartments. They wholeheartedly embrace the language of 'themes', 'style', 'characterisation' and the rest.

Consider, for example, this passage from Brodie's *Tess of the D'Urbevilles*:[9]

> Finally, the impact of a story depends on its style. If an author has nothing worth saying, he has failed before he has begun: but even when he has a great deal to say, but lacks the secret of conveying it in a way to make an impression upon his readers, he has failed no less.

The division between the 'theme' and the author's 'treatment' of it is absolute. What is particularly interesting, however, in the light of the examiners' complaints about candidates who fail to address themselves to matters of style is the phrase that is used to refer to the author's technique. It is seen as a 'secret'. The notion that an author's style should be approached with reverence because it is mysterious perhaps explains why 'A' level students remain convinced that books are full of 'hidden meanings'. It is interesting to reflect that what might be called professional criticism ignores categories of this kind, and the vocabulary that goes with them.

Despite their strictures – 'there are still far too many candidates who attempt an ill-fitting adaptation of prepared work on a topic, or of published "Notes"'[10] and 'Poetry, yet again was largely a matter of themes'[11] – most examination papers are firmly fixed in the same tradition. And, as a consequence, many questions are couched in terms that, because they are reductive, distort and inhibit meaningful critical response. This is JMB: 'The study of literature depends upon an awareness of style as well as content, and the reduction of texts to tracts limits the success of the answers.' The problem that arises when it is put like this, of course, is that the phraseology reinforces the very distinctions that it claims to deplore. The form or genre becomes least visible when it is suggested that the work might have an existence (content) independent of the language in which it is embodied (style).

An easy target for this kind of criticism is the question that asks candidates to 'put one of the following passages into good, modern English prose'.[12] This sort of invitation to paraphrase, however, is becoming something of a rarity, and even when it was more commonplace, it commanded only a very small proportion of the marks. Much more significant are the kind of questions that almost unwittingly reveal a widely held set of assumptions about how writers write. These questions commonly assume that the author – any author – having selected a *theme*, then decorates it with a variety of literary *effects* that will make it *interesting* to the reader.

The term 'theme' is used to describe just about everything from the broadest categorization of poetry ('the themes of love and religious experience . . . in metaphysical poetry'),[13] to the sensibility of the writer ('the theme of changing fortunes' in Chaucer),[14] to the fabric of the fictional world ('the theme of social distinction in *The Winter's Tale*').[15] Whatever way it is employed, it has the effect of isolating a specific aspect of the work and suggesting that, in some way, it pre-dates the act of composition.

Having selected a 'theme', however, the writer moves on to the next stage, in which literary techniques are chosen, on the basis of whether they are appropriate or not, and used to create the poem, play or novel. The key word here is 'used'. Writers do not, for example, have a comic vision, they 'use satire and comic irony' (Chaucer),[16] they do not draw on a language whose meaning is shaped by social and historical forces greater than themselves, they 'make varied uses of Nature' (Marvell),[17] and they do not think in metaphysical terms, they 'use conceits' (Donne).[18] As with the indiscriminate use of the term 'theme', the effect is to reinforce critical procedures that dismantle the work of Art. What we are required to imagine is a kind of literary assembly line.

The reason for selecting these devices is to achieve 'various effects' (Shakespeare's sonnets),[19] 'to create a dramatic effect' (Chaucer),[20] or to work up 'dramatic interest' (Shakespeare and Eliot).[21] It is a minimalist view of how readers or audiences respond to literature. It suggests that the writer's task is to satisfy jaded appetites with literary tricks – the author as Scheherezade.

The reduction of literature to a rag-bag of tricks and devices does not even do justice to writers for whom matters of technique are an absorbing preoccupation. Offered to 'A' level students as a universal critical model, it is not only seriously misleading, it also, ironically, reinforces all the weaknesses that are identified in the examiners' reports.

3 Literature II: . . . and practice

The picture of how the subject is taught that has been painted in the preceding chapters has been sufficiently alarming for some explanation to be required of how any 16-year-old actually makes it to the end of the course. The obstacles seem insurmountable. The main thing to remember is that the subject only looks incoherent at the level of underlying principle; on the surface everything is fine. Indeed, English Literature continues to attract one of the largest entries among 'A' level subjects and schools are apparently very successful at achieving good results. The mistake is to think that a curriculum must be coherent to be successful. There are a great many other considerations more decisive than that. Indeed, almost any pedagogic practice that is backed by custom and practice is likely to carry greater influence than the most elegantly rational piece of curriculum planning. English teachers are very good at papering over the cracks.

Before going into any more detail about how the illusion is managed, some mention should be made of the casualties of the system, those for whom it does not work. It should not be forgotten that the reassuring statistics about entry and pass rates do not tell us anything about the students that failed to reach the starting post. Anecdotal evidence, particularly from colleges of further education, but also from sixth-form colleges, suggests that the drop-out rate can be quite high, and while there are a number of explanations for this, the possibility should not be discounted that it may have something to do with the shortcomings of the syllabuses on offer. One of the reasons why 'new' sixth formers have posed less of a challenge to the curriculum than the Schools Council anticipated when it promoted the N and F proposals may be that they simply melted away in the face of the status quo.

What this chapter is primarily concerned with, however, is the way in which custom and practice have conspired to create the seamless garment of 'A' level English. It is about how, when a sticky label marked 'literature' is slapped on a book, the rules change about how it must be read. It is about how this simple device allows the curriculum to remain firmly the property of the teacher, and it is about how this ensures that pupils will learn to do what they are told whether they understand what they are doing or not.

Papering over the cracks

In *Literary Theory: An Introduction*, Terry Eagleton (1983) argues that 'Literary theorists, critics and teachers . . . are not so much purveyors of doctrine as custodians of a discourse', and 'certain pieces of writing are selected as being more amenable to this discourse than others, and these are what is known as literature or the literary canon'. In the selection of books as 'A' level set texts, it is possible to observe something very similar taking place.

Although the 'A' level canon is no longer confined to 'the classics', examiners continue to be preoccupied with 'literary greatness', howsoever that may be defined. The rule of thumb would appear to be that a work of literature has to demonstrate a feeling for 'enduring human values'. Only then is it likely to be of sufficient 'weight' and 'complexity'. It follows that the genius of the author resides in his (for it usually is) ability to defy the constraints of time and place.

The hallmark of quality in a writer is the ability to survey the contemporary scene and distinguish between what is ephemeral and what is eternal. The 'ephemeral' usually covers anything to do with politics, economics or popular culture. Indeed, the canon is indifferent to any kind of experience that is not intrinsically 'significant' or capable of being made to seem so.

This point is more important than it might seem. The line between what is significant in literary terms and what has status in social terms is a thin one, often transgressed by those seeking to define the limits of the canon. Hence the exclusion of all kinds of categories of writing on the grounds that they are idiosyncratic or unrepresentative. What they have failed to represent, of course, is the experience of the dominant social group.

The demand that works of literature appeal for confirmation of their excellence over the head, as it were, of the society in which they were created, has a curious effect. It compels the reader to look for some kind of correspondence with the words on the page, irrespective of whether one exists. At one and the same time, it seeks to establish that writers are unique and that they can uncannily find common cause with us. It almost invites literature to be judged not on its merits but on its ability to reflect twentieth-century concerns. At 'A' level, this line of reasoning is well represented, not least in examination questions that ask whether the set text is capable of 'speaking to a modern audience'.

It might be argued that practice has changed dramatically over the last 15 years, so that syllabuses now encourage the study of a much greater variety of texts. The inclusion of contemporary literature in the set book lists is no longer even mildly controversial. Indeed, the precedents are so well established that as well as authors like William Golding whose work is obviously weighty, it is possible for 'A' level students to study writers whose claims to be 'modern classics' are probably rather more slender.

Whatever the credentials of the books it is processing, however, the literary machine grinds on. Consider what happens once a book of this kind has been singled out for study. Here is a question on *Catch 22*:

> What positive values, if any, does Heller present through the character of Yossarian in Catch 22? Illustrate in detail from the novel. (JMB 1985)

What is immediately obvious about the question is the assumption that it makes about literary judgements. 'Positive values' in novels are a 'good thing', full stop. Arguably, the reason why the question has been asked in this way is that the examiner had doubts about whether *Catch 22* was really suitable for inclusion in the canon. 'Positive values', after all, are not a stone's throw away from Leavisite notions about literature being 'vitalizing' or 'life enhancing'. Anybody who thinks that the examination boards have jettisoned their traditional values is wrong. In casting the net rather more widely for the selection of set books at 'A' level, the examiners are seeking not to fragment, but to reinforce the canon.

The consequences of allowing judgements of this kind to determine the selection of set books should not be underestimated. Teachers are forced into a kind of tunnel vision, for only by ignoring the extent to which meaning is socially constructed can they continue to isolate literature as a special case, capable of being studied without reference to anything else. These assumptions contribute further towards the sense of bewilderment felt by students unused to the way in which academic study quarantines whole areas of intellectual enquiry.

It means that much of the reading they might choose for themselves – Catherine Cookson, for example, or Stephen King – is illicit, and, therefore, unworthy of serious consideration. Equally out of bounds are all the other kinds of writing (and indeed speech) that play a crucial part in the process whereby words accrue meaning. As a consequence, the books that these students are required to read – the works of literature – have to be judged and, indeed, understood, by proxy.

They become part of a category of books about which *literary* questions are asked and *literary* answers provided. Students quickly learn that their previous experience of reading is no longer of value, and that they must become novices again. This has the singular effect of putting them entirely at the mercy of their teachers, and inhibiting them from asking awkward questions. It effectively disables them.

A greater understanding of how this actually works in practice emerges from a look at one of the major conventions of question-setting at 'A' level. One kind of question appears on exam papers more frequently than any other. All of the exam boards use it, and all of them seem equally oblivious to its shortcomings. By jamming the word 'discuss' on to the end of an all-purpose quote, teachers and examiners alike seem to believe that they can transform the most banal comment into an interesting talking point, while simultaneously ducking out of any responsibility for the opinions that are being expressed.

To be fair, the intention is a quite different and thoroughly commendable one.

Questions of this kind appeal because they seem to offer a way of provoking comment without either predetermining or pre-empting the candidate's own opinion. They look like the perfect device for encouraging a genuinely personal response, while leaving a few necessary constraints in place to help the least confident.

Closer attention to their form, however, suggests that a very different message can sometimes be conveyed. It is a mistake to think of this kind of question as open-ended. It is by no means difficult to provide a wording that excludes from the invitation to 'discuss' key concepts that may be highly controversial. Take this question from the JMB paper 2 (1985):

> The Duchess of Malfi is no more than a series of events designed to please the lowest tastes of an audience. Discuss.

It is informed by a value judgement that, whatever twists and turns might be employed in justifying the question, simply is not made contentious by the addition of 'discuss'. The candidate is offered, as fact, a moral universe that, ironically, is itself put under the microscope in Webster's play. The assumptions about 'high art' and 'low' tastes are unassailable. Something similar is taking place in the question set, in the same year, on *Othello*:

> Othello is a play of violent contrasts, of language, character and mood. Discuss these and any other contrasts you have found in the play.[1]

There is not much room here to ask whether *Othello* actually is a play of 'violent contrasts' or whether it might mean anything at all to suggest that it is. The candidate is given the daunting task of 'discussing' something that provides little scope for offering a point of view. Far from provoking a response, this question merely encourages candidates to reach for their stock of prepared answers.

When the Ministry of Education in Ontario, Canada, recently reformed the provincial examinations for 18-year-olds, they mounted a major in-service programme to accompany the introduction of the Ontario Academic Courses (OAC). Because a significant part of the course is now teacher-assessed, special attention was paid to the phrasing of essay questions. This is what the teachers' handbook had to say about the word 'discuss':

> In particular, the word 'discuss', found on all the examinations in the 1983–84 investigation, is a landmine of ambiguity. Students see the word as an invitation to respond in a variety of ways. Teachers who argue that such variety is acceptable would have no consistency of response from student to student, and hence no basis of comparison for students' performances.

Included in the booklet was an appendix which quoted from a survey of student interpretations of the word:

> Show or prove by explanation

> Discuss means explain, in my own words using an introduction and conclusion to the statement. In the body, I would put in a few points and relate them to the story to prove or disprove the statement.

Discuss means to analyse in depth.

Discuss means to present analogies and comparisons and through their juxtapositions come to a conclusion based on evidence.

Discuss means to explain fully what is meant by the statement.

Discuss means to talk about, to show how different events are related.

Discuss means to put down facts with evidence that supports them.

Discuss means to talk about the importance of character, plot etc.

Discuss means to analyse, covering the question from every possible angle.

Discuss means to write as much as you can about something using examples to illustrate.

Discuss means to say everything you know about whatever is asked.

Discuss means to present all the facts and express both sides of the argument and give your personal opinion.

At first sight there does not seem to be much to choose between one interpretation and another. A closer reading, however, reveals quite important differences of emphasis. Some of the responses are, themselves, ambiguous, but where it is possible to be reasonably certain, a clear distinction emerges between those who think that you can enter into a dispute with the quotation (e.g. 'give your personal opinion' or 'come to a conclusion') and those who do not (e.g. 'to prove by explanation' or 'to explain fully what is meant').

What is alarming is the absence of any definition which even recognizes as a possibility that the question itself may need to be taken apart. The third comment ('Discuss means to analyse in depth') might carry that interpretation but, in all probability, it is the text that is being recommended for analysis, not the question.

An even more disturbing feature of the invitation to 'discuss', however, is the tendency for the quote to become a kind of critical cameo that demands to be imitated. By encompassing some reasonably central or major aspect of the text in a brief, self-explanatory quote, the question validates the generalization at the expense of the particular. It frames one reader's response with quotation marks in such a way that all readers are distanced from the text. It suggests that there is more value in the dispassionate than in the committed. This question on Chaucer illustrates the point neatly:

> Despite the vitality of the narrative, we never, even for a half line, lose sight of the narrator of The Pardoner's Tale. Discuss.[2]

The assumption that the experience of one reader is the experience of all readers ('we') may be a familiar one, but it can create a sense of dislocation between the individual and the book they have read. It introduces an army of other readers, all marching in time to the music, all evidence that texts have only one meaning and that critical disagreements are simply the way we get there.

Judgements about complex literary texts that can be captured in one or two well chosen phrases will inevitably tend to suggest that the work is a seamless and consistent whole. When the candidate attempts to come to terms with judgements delivered in this way, they have little choice but to share the same assumption. For many 18-year-olds, this is a daunting task.

The effect is to make them reliant upon received wisdom for any kind of response to literature, able to answer questions only by reference to some kind of training in what is expected of them. It fuels the suspicion that the exam exists not to foster critical enquiry or literary response, but to initiate candidates into the conventions of literary criticism.

If this is the case, then there is an easy answer to the question asked earlier about how the system works. Students will jump through endless hoops, however meaningless, if what is being expected of them can be presented as a rite of passage. What they learn to attach to the procedures associated with literary criticism is, if you like, a ritual rather than an actual significance.

The final point that needs to be made about how the cracks are papered over recalls an earlier section on assessment. It was suggested that the 'A' level exam experiences some quite reasonable difficulties in trying to distinguish between what candidates say and the way they say it. The solution to this problem, however, leaves the examiners in a very uncomfortable position since it leaves the unmistakable impression that they have no real interest in how students read.

This is certainly a fair reflection of the dilemma described in the examiners' report for the University of London Board (1981). In commenting on the quality of the work submitted for examination, the authors of the report make their judgements according to some very revealing criteria. Having discussed the way in which candidates had interpreted a question on Jane Austen, they make the general comment that 'overall, there was much fine writing here'. Later, in the same report, they observe about paper III (Unseen Criticism), that 'In many ways, this is the paper where some of the most interesting and exciting writing occurs.'

What is immediately striking about these comments is that, rather than sensitivity of literary response, they both stress, as a significant feature of the assessment procedure, the quality of the candidate's prose style. With these two passages flashing like warning lights, the whole report can be read for its preoccupation with how the candidates write rather than what they have to say. The opening paragraph, for example, introduces most of the criteria that are later formalized in a 'profile' of the general assessment criteria in marking the scripts:

> Much excellent work was produced in this first examination on the new syllabus. There was often a pleasing knowledge of the texts, indicated by brief and apt quotation and sometimes supported by relevant comment from critics, and there was exciting writing which showed verve and sensitivity.

Knowledge, received opinion and prose style, these are what will be rewarded in a kind of linguistic beauty contest. The 'profile' is similarly dominated by consideration of *how* candidates have answered the question, at the expense of any attention to what they may have to say (see Table 1).

Table 1. Profile

Criteria	Good	Average	Weak
Relevance Coverage of points raised by the question	Full. Will note subtlety, complexities and possible disagreements: will discuss	More relaxed application. May follow obvious line: uncritically accepts the terms of the question	May ignore question. Thin, inadequate, incomplete. The updated, prepared answer
Content Use of text	Full, relevant and incisive, with sufficient and apt example	Moderately full. Still relevant but perhaps implicitly so. Less controlled and applied	Irrelevance; narration, summary or account. Incompleteness
Structure The order and logic of the argument	Progressive, pertinent, focused, convincing, well instructed	Argument should be evident, but probably less controlled and purposeful. May plod a bit	Confused, even non-existent
Style The quality of the expression	Clear, incisive, correct, even elegant	Ordinary, comprehensible, perhaps rather colourless	Slack, incorrect, possibly inappropriate

In practice, it seems, the examiners are less relentlessly scrupulous about avoiding literary judgements, and, as a consequence, the relationship between the general criteria described at the beginning of the report and some of the detailed observations contained within it is an uneasy one. What, for example, are we to make of the fact that 'Chaucer evoked lively and engaged responses', or that 'those who tackled Donne' often did so 'with insight and flair'? Both judgements should, perhaps, have been dismissed as evidence of a dangerous subjectivity on the part of the examiner.

The inexperienced reader

It is one thing to look at 'A' level Literature from the point of view of the teacher, another to try to appreciate how it feels as a student. This section, then, which takes a look at the plight of the inexperienced reader, is rather more speculative, and incomplete. It is intended as a way of hazarding a guess about how the subject appears to a student who finds the language of literary discourse unfamiliar and perplexing.

All 'A' level teachers will recognize the moment at which a teaching group can, for no explicable reason, take leave of its senses, and offer interpretations that are so obtuse as to be baffling. The following is an extract from the JMB examiner's report of 1984. It describes responses to *Dover Beach*, set as the unseen poem for Paper III:

> Far more unexpected and disturbing was the failure of so many [candidates] to form even the remotest idea of what the poem is about . . . some interpretations were extraordinary. More than half of the panel of examiners remarked on the frequency with which Arnold was supposed to be writing about, or involved in, the D-Day landings, on the strength of associations prompted, no doubt, by this summer's ceremonies, with 'French coast', 'beach' and armies clashing on a darkling plain. At the root of what one examiner felicitously described as these 'wild games of "hunt the theme"' lay simple failure to recognise that 'the sea of faith' – which, to be fair, many sensed to be crucial to any understanding of the poem – is a metaphor.

It is fairly evident what has happened. Prompted partly no doubt by the panic induced by examination conditions, but also by the conviction that poetry is eccentric, these candidates have found themselves in a position which quite simply does not allow them to use their intelligence. They have no way of making the words mean anything, so they are trying to read the poem as if they were somebody else, somebody who understood it. Their faulty appreciation of how poetry works can be traced back to a curriculum that fails to offer any meaningful version of how language works. It should not come as much of a surprise to discover that figurative language stays mysterious if there is no comparable experience of any other kind of language, or if such experiences are devalued because they are not literary. What these students have discovered during their 'A' level course is that there is one set of things to be said about literature, and another about books that you read for pleasure. Indeed, it is highly probable that they have managed to construct two different and competing value systems which co-exist with each other. That so many students seem quite capable of managing this is a tribute to how effectively our education system prepares people for the mastery of double standards. None the less, it does create difficulties, largely because, by establishing a whole category of writing in which meaning is divorced from its social and historical context, it separates judgement from experience. What happens sooner or later is what happened with *Dover Beach* – students are simply overwhelmed.

At the risk of repetition it is worth retracing the path that leads to this confusion. For many students their first experience of 'A' level English will be a teacher telling them that from now on things will be done differently. While the intention may be admirable, the effect can be bewildering. What the teacher no doubt means is that the students will now be treated more like adults. What the students understand is that they can forget their hard won experience. Post-GCSE, they may well be told, books will be more 'difficult', and critical approaches will be more 'rigorous'.

Even when teachers do not make their intentions explicit in this way, they are similarly engaged in providing students with a vocabulary that allows them to talk about different kinds of books in different ways. Characteristically, they will be expecting students to adopt a more 'objective' analytical approach, the implication being that only in this way is it possible to establish what a book 'means'.

It will not be long, however, before the students discover that not only do members of their 'A' level group disagree with each other, but so do eminent critics. While the much vaunted objectivity of their newly acquired critical procedures is made to seem a sham, they remain, because of the language now at their command, inhibited about trusting their own response. The only way in which they can reconcile these conflicting versions of what they are doing is by seeing it all as quite unmanageable, since most of them, if forced to decide whether 'Eng. Lit.' is nonsense or hard, will plump for it being hard. After all, the notion that it might be nonsense is actually much more threatening.

As they progress through the course, they will also begin to discover for themselves that apparently open examination questions conceal a hidden agenda, and they will soon learn to agonize about whether their answers are 'right' or not. When they are entreated to trust their own response, they will fall silent, since experience may well have taught them to do quite the opposite. Eventually, they will manage to transform each set book into a collection of notes that will see them through the exam. For the unseen paper, which they will approach in fear and trembling, they will simply keep their fingers crossed and hope it is not *Dover Beach*. But it will be.

Not all students, of course, will experience problems of this kind. For the initiated, those likely to go on and read English in higher education, say, the dislocation between what they think they are doing and what they are actually doing is much less painful. These students will almost certainly be capable of pursuing intellectual enquiry without commitment. A small number may be impatient with what they see as playing games, but most will happily accept that the apprentice may also be the dilettante. For others, however, perhaps more earnest, perhaps, for reasons to do with class and background, more uncompromising in judging the value of what they are doing, the contradictions of liberal criticism can be experienced as a puzzle that is bewildering rather than engaging. Far from being a challenge, it will invite only despair.

4 Literature III: the alternatives

Had *Dover Beach* been put in front of an 'A' level group by a teacher rather than set on a question paper by an examiner, it might have evoked a different response. It is not difficult to imagine the desperate surmising reported by the JMB, the wild stabs in the dark inspired by the need to get something down on paper, being replaced in the classroom by a baffled silence. In such circumstances, few students will willingly admit their failure to understand what is being required by the invitation to comment on the poem. And those that are sufficiently self-confident to do so present their teachers with a real problem. The obvious response, and the one adopted by most teachers most of the time, is to rephrase the instruction. Offered this solution, most students will instantly feign understanding and turn back to the printed page with an expression of deep concentration. For both student and teacher, it is a necessary assumption that the difficulty can be traced back to some relatively trivial matter of wording. What they can both accept is an occasional lapse in pedagogic technique, with the important proviso that such lapses are never sufficiently serious for anybody to imagine that the teacher's competence has been challenged. To acknowledge anything else, e.g. that the rules of the critical enquiry in which the group is engaged are culturally specific and, therefore, more accessible to some students than to others, would be unthinkable. The whole enterprise would be put at risk.

The evidence of the 'Alternative' syllabuses in English suggests that teachers who are aware of this problem and willing to do something about it, remain none the less committed to the same basic belief that the difficulties can be overcome by more imaginative teaching and more flexible systems of assessment. The problem is still perceived as being essentially about pedagogic technique.

In making this point, it is hard to avoid seeming dismissive. That is not the intention. The new syllabuses must rank as some of the most exciting developments that have been seen since the introduction of 'A' level in 1951. None the less, it is important not to blur the issue when considering what makes them innovative. They can be embraced with equal enthusiasm by the most entrenched Leavisite and the most wild-eyed structuralist. The point is that they provide an opportunity to teach in a different way, rather than to promote a different critical ideology.

Almost the only attempt that has been made systematically to gather information about 'alternative' syllabuses at 'A' level 'English' is Bill Greenwell's excellent *Alternatives at English 'A' level* (1988). Modestly, he only allows himself an Appendix in which to express his 'personal view'. He is less than overwhelmed:

> . . . the innovations recorded in this handbook add up to comparatively little. What is most striking is the conservatism of boards and teachers about the subject of English Literature, and the manner of examining it. But the 45 minute essay, the global question, the recourse to received judgements in the science of literary criticism, the concept of practical criticism – all these have not been with teachers and pupils since the beginning of time. They are mainly late educational arrivals. Yet they are treated as admirable fossils. Many of the 'alternative' syllabuses are mutton dressed up as more palatable lamb. Hence the inverted commas around the word 'alternative' in the sub-title to this booklet.

This is a little disingenuous. Elsewhere, he shows real enthusiasm for some of the opportunities provided by course work, open book exams, the extended essay, personal writing and the rest. However, the point is well made.

Any attempt like Bill Greenwell's to summarize changes in the examination system inevitably stresses that which can most readily be specified – systems of assessment, the weighting of different sections of the syllabus, categories for different kinds of assignment and the like. Equally important, though easily missed in the welter of statistics, are the reasons why so many teachers have abandoned the traditional syllabuses. *Alternatives at English 'A' level* estimates that between 1981 and 1985 'the proportion of candidates including an alternative element in their syllabus doubled' and calculates that in 1985 'alternative' candidates formed roughly 10 per cent of the total. Since then his 'best estimate is that they have . . . doubled again'. It is a quite remarkable success story.

Part of the reason why it has happened is because of changing perceptions about what takes place when a student encounters a text. The *Dover Beach* problem is increasingly being seen as typical rather than aberrant. Teachers have become much more willing to accept the view that students are inexperienced readers and that 'A' level courses need to be more sensitive towards their developmental needs. Some of the key features of this approach can be summarized as follows:

1 *Reading is an active process. The reader is an active creator of meaning, not a passive recipient of language.* What this highlights is the importance of 'response', a key concept, of course, in GCSE English Literature. Students will more readily understand what they are reading if they are engaged in it. Appreciation and understanding by themselves are not enough.

2 *The meaning of a text for any individual depends as much on what is brought to it as upon what is contained within it.* By implication, students are likely to become more sophisticated readers if they have the opportunity to choose their own

texts or if the teacher has the freedom to establish a programme of reading more suited to the individual student's interests and aspirations.

3 *Reading is not a single skill which once acquired can be employed in all circumstances with equal ease. Some kinds of reading are more demanding than others.* This point has been conceded as GCSE, but its relevance is less widely accepted at 'A' level. Teachers are giving more thought, for example, to questions about how and when students should be asked to make generalizations about a text, or how close reading can most profitably be employed.

4 *Texts do not immediately yield up meaning. Their significance for any individual is different on different occasions, and can alter as a result of reflection and discussion.* Many works of literature are specifically designed to resist the instant response; traditional systems of assessment have never recognized this.

It is difficult to embrace a view of reading like this – one that lays such stress on the reader – while continuing to enter students for 'sudden death' exams on prescribed texts. The only way of solving the problem is by opting for more flexible systems of assessment – course work or 'open book'. And of the two, it is the 'open book' exam that can be the most potent agent for change, particularly when it is in the hands of a group of examiners who know exactly what they want. This is how Bill Greenwell describes the approach adopted by the JMB:

Some of the syllabuses – notably the JMB/Sheffield syllabus – set out to encourage a diversity of response to the language of literature by prescribing and describing identifiably different kinds of response.

A similar impulse inspires the 'open book' paper developed by the AEB in its 'Alternative' syllabus (660).[1] The questions illustrate how, even within the constraints of a timed examination, it is possible to change quite dramatically the relationship between examiner, text and student. By comparison with the stern injunctions and the austere prose of their predecessors, these 'alternative' examiners are positively chatty. The AEB paper set in 1986, for example, invites candidates to 'try to define' the changes in atmosphere in *The Winter's Tale*.[2] It suggests, in a question on 'Emma', that 'it might be a good idea to select three passages in order to give some flavour of the novel',[3] and it bases a question about *The Grapes of Wrath* on 'The "blurb" on the back of the Pan edition'.[4] The persistent use of the second person, as in 'How has Pinter evoked these reactions in you?',[5] is a clear indication that what matters is response. In the conventional syllabuses, 'you' only get a mention as somebody capable of judiciously weighing up what 'we' feel. In the AEB open book paper, your reactions have some value on their own merits. This is not just an empty rhetorical device. The paper is full of suggestions about how you might read the text ('What can you deduce . . .'), or structure your answer ('Make clear which parts you are choosing . . .'), all of which provide a sharp contrast with the kind of traditional question that grew visibly nervous after the second line about whether too much was being given away.

Perhaps of greater significance than this, however, is the type of question that open book papers tend to promote. By inviting candidates to focus on a particular chapter or scene and write about how it 'prepares the reader for what follows' or 'reflects themes important to the play as a whole', these questions make it difficult to maintain the kind of disembodied 'version' of a text that is so characteristic of conventional syllabuses. They demand a much greater sensitivity towards language, a greater focus on the particular.

One indication of how influential this style of question setting can be is contained in the examiner's report on paper 1 for the same year:

> One assistant examiner made a very helpful point about empathy and identification. Partly because of the nature of the Smith poem and the Lawrence passage he felt that a lot of candidates were 'feeling that they were there', smelling the flowers and touching the stones, many of them 'relating to' and 'identifying with'. This sometimes sounded like overpleading, patting the author too heartily on the back. He drew a distinction between empathy and standing alongside a character and the kind of wholesale identification of half pretending to be the author. Perhaps it might be helpful to think about discussing what kind of involvement is created when one reads a piece of literature when the writer is transmitting feelings and involving readers in experience. It might be useful to explore the nature of the imaginative experience of the reader. When the three phrases quoted above appeared most frequently, there was often a sense that the candidate was in fact not 'relating to' or 'identifying with' but using these phrases as a kind of evasive short cut, not examining the nature of how exactly the writer had conveyed experience to the reader.

Although these observations are intended primarily as practical guidance for teachers, they raise a number of broader issues.

What evidently has taken place is something along the following lines. Frustrated by the failure of students to make sense of what they are reading, teachers have sought to develop a new pedagogy which attempts to replicate for the student some of the close relationship with a text that most adult readers take for granted, but which is, in fact, a consequence of their maturity and education. The label attached to this, 'response', may seem to indicate only what a student does after reading a text (i.e. discuss it, write about it, etc.), but this is a misleading impression. Of equal importance in eliciting a considered response is the choice of text, and the circumstances under which it is read.

However, this approach which started life as part of the professional baggage of teachers who, for professional reasons, have a well-developed sense of the importance of what is happening to the reader, has refused to stay obediently in the pigeon hole marked 'teaching techniques'. To the extent that a subject is its methodology, changes in one will inevitably spill over into the other. One misconception, that literature is a way of dressing up ideas in figurative language, has been replaced by another, that literature is about recreating experience as faithfully as possible.

Something similar happens when the teacher consciously pursues a policy that is designed to turn students into active readers. Here is John Parry writing in *English 'A' Level in Practice* (Post-14 Committee, 1988):

> An active engagement with words on the page means that the student literally makes something of the text. A passive acceptance of the teacher's views means that the student is permanently distanced from the book.

With this as his starting point, John Parry produces an 'A to Z of creative exercises for A-level English Literature', pulling one idea after another out of his capacious hat. It is a *tour de force*, but he recognizes the dangers:

> Casting Macbeth, Lady Macbeth and the witches (Pamela Stephenson? Patricia Hayes?) raises fundamental questions about characters' appearance and reality. Director of Theatr Clwyd, George Roman, decided that Macbeth must be 30, because this is the age when the walls start closing in and you become set for middle age, or you branch out, say, into being a great train robber. *We don't want to replace 'How many children had Lady Macbeth?' with 'How old was she?'* but it can reveal interesting Shakespearean detail, if closely tied to the evidence in the text.

What John Parry alerts his readers to is the danger that the imaginative classroom device capable of enthusing students, might turn literature into a kind of up-market 'Dungeons and Dragons'.

It is this lack of certainty about where the subject ends and the pedagogic techniques associated with it begin, that has made it difficult to see the alternative syllabuses for what they are. Because they have been prompted by a more sophisticated understanding of how to develop higher-order reading skills, it might have been thought that the new syllabuses were also making a point about how the meaning of a literary text is not simply embodied in the words on the page.

In practice, connections of this kind appear not to have been made, and approaches to text have been fairly conventional. The alternative syllabuses have been used not to redefine English studies but to provide a more efficient system for achieving quite conventional goals. The world has been made safe again for Leavisite criticism. Consider this extract from an essay published in *Personal Response – A Selection of Coursework Assignments* by the JMB Sheffield special syllabus group:

> 'Hughes' most significant theme is the central opposition between the vital, instinctive impulse of birds and animals, often violent and destructive, and the dulled or tamed consciousness of over-civilised people or passive animals'. Discuss this view of Hughes' early poetry with reference to at least four poems.
>
> *One poem which illustrates the instinctive, vital impulse of birds is 'Thrushes'. In it Hughes uncovers the reality behind the image of these birds. They are not small, fragile birds, but aggressive, and even instinctive killers within their own environment. The first and second verses of the poem describe the thrushes almost as automatons of 'coiled steel' which are subjected to being 'triggered to stirrings'. Hughes uses the rhythm of the poem to illustrate this*

in that they 'start', 'bounce', and 'stab', monosyllabic words which suggest an emotionless, instinctive kill.

The thrushes are closely integrated with precision. They are 'sleek' and possess a 'dark deadly eye'. There are 'no sighs or headscratchings', no unsurety or doubt, but pure instinct. An inbuilt mechanism of destruction seems almost to exist within the thrushes. Their 'bullet and automatic purpose' cannot be attributed to either their single mindedness, their trained bodies, or their genius; it is a natural instinct, an inbuilt function, which both Mozart's brain and the shark's mouth possess. The thrushes are compared to the shark which is too so highly developed in its mechanism of killing that it will devour itself at smelling its own blood, ultimate efficiency.

The precision of these birds is so highly developed that it leaves no room for doubt or obstruction, problems which plague man. Because man is so inefficient his actions are often doubted by his brain. Therefore he must make choices. He must choose between good and evil, a problem which the thrushes do not face, for they know that they are perfect.

Thus the insignificance of man is illustrated in that these small creatures are more secure and confident than himself. Man needs to feel that he has achieved something, whether visible or spiritual, in order to accept himself and gain fulfilment. He needs to perform his 'heroisms on horseback' or carve at a 'tiny ivory ornament', or outstrip his desk diary, thus endeavouring to prove himself superior to the world around him. Man displays a certain degree of frivolity in displaying a futile superiority in trying to prove himself more worthy than useless, inanimate objects such as the desk diary; this is the extent of his feelings of inferiority.

The thrushes possess a natural killer instinct; they kill for food and they do it by means of their own bodies. Man, however, has no need to kill unaided anyway; he needs weapons to instill in him a feeling of security, thus showing his inferiority. The 'moral' of this poem may be that looks are deceptive; the pretty, harmless birds are actually automated killers, the self-confident humans are in fact insecure and pathetic.

There's nothing here that is not immediately familiar. The question firmly establishes the boundaries of the critical enquiry with its reference to 'significant themes', boundaries that the student gratefully accepts – 'the "moral" of the poem may be . . .'. Nor is it any accident that the 'themes' are 'significant' ones. Subtly, the poetry is being incorporated into the canon. Hughes is placed in the tradition of English nature poetry, his reflections on the nature of existence legitimized, and consequently protected from any kind of searching scrutiny. It is not surprising that when the student actually starts to write about the poem, she has little choice but to elucidate the text, throwing in a few observations about Hughes' poetic technique ('the rhythm' established by his 'monosyllabic words'). Indeed, so determined is she to impose a reassuring coherence on the poem that she even irons out Hughes' own, presumably ironic, 'head-scratchings'. This is what he writes at the beginning of the second verse:

> Is it their single-mind-sized skulls, or a trained
> Body, or genius, or a nestful of brats
> Gives their days this bullet and automatic
> Purpose?

It is glossed as if no question has been asked, or, at least, as if the question that is asked had been unequivocally answered:

> Their 'bullet and automatic purpose' cannot be attributed to either their single-mindedness, their trained bodies, or their genius; it is a natural instinct, an inbuilt function, which both Mozart's brain and the shark's mouth possess.

It is a similar desire to sustain a sense of the thematic unity of the poem that leads this student to neglect the difficult final lines, with their apocalyptic language:

> . . . how loud and above what
> Furious spaces of fire do the distracting devils
> Orgy and hosannah . . .

The critical model to which she is working is not one that readily allows any uncertainty about meaning, or admits the possibility that a poem may be both good and incoherent.

The point of this analysis is not to belittle this student's achievement – indeed she has done well what was asked of her – but to illustrate how, in practice, it is quite easy to embrace the philosophy of the 'alternative' syllabuses, while remaining firmly in the mainstream of critical enquiry. A more radical approach only becomes possible by ditching altogether the idea of English Literature as a discrete syllabus. And one way of doing this is to start not with Literature, but with Language.

5 Language I: language study or linguistics?

The notion that 'A' level might include 'a systematic study of the language' first surfaced in 1964 with the publication of the Lockwood Report:

> The type of course we have in mind would include a study of the structure of the language; the different types of English, the position of standard English, dialects and slang; and the relation of language to individual thought and behaviour and also its social implications.

It is quite clear from the report itself that this proposal was not lightly made. The committee appended a specimen syllabus and question paper, and must have had hopes that their blueprint, or something like it, would be adopted by one or other of the Examining Boards. Why it should take 20 years for their hopes to be realized is an interesting matter for speculation. The conventional view is that the Lockwood proposals were too demanding, both for the students that it was anticipated might follow the course, and the teachers who might teach it. While there might be room for disagreement about how well the students would have coped, there is probably some justification for the view that their teachers, almost exclusively trained as literary critics, would have struggled.

None the less, this explanation is by no means totally convincing. If the only problem with the Lockwood proposals had been that they were too demanding, then a solution could easily have been found. After all, it is not difficult to take a list of linguistic concepts and adjust them however you wish according to perceptions about what an 18-year-old can be expected to understand. What cannot so easily be supplied is a confident sense of the proper relationship between academic linguistics and the school curriculum. And without that, what teachers lack is far more important than linguistic expertise. Without that, they have no firm basis for making decisions about whether, or where, such a study should be included in the curriculum, and they have no means of deciding what kind of teaching might be appropriate. It is scarcely surprising that the Lockwood initiative gathered dust.

In the 20 years that followed the publication of the Lockwood Report, these issues provided a central strand in the wider debate about the nature and purposes of English teaching. It would be idle to pretend that, by 1984, they were so completely resolved that 'A' level English Language could emerge blinking into the light of day. Indeed, both of the syllabuses currently on offer represent a different resolution of the problem. None the less, an important change had taken place. Put crudely, 'A' level itself was beginning to be seen as a part of the school curriculum, and not simply as a preparation for higher education. Once it is acknowledged that schooling may finish at 19, as well as 16 or 21, then space in the sixth-form curriculum has to be justified in other ways, by reference, say, to vocational or personal needs. It makes no sense at all to cite practice in higher education. What starts to matter are the same things that have mattered from the age of 5. As a consequence, the spectre of 'A' level Linguistics could be firmly dismissed and due attention be given to the more important question of how language should be studied when it is freed from the need to ape its related academic discipline.

For this reason, it is important that the two 'A' level English Language syllabuses, from London (1981) and JMB (1983), are situated in the wider debate about 'knowledge about language'. In that context, it is possible to be aware of the whole range of questions that need to be addressed and not to become mesmerized by the single issue of linguistic orthodoxy.

That debate was well-established long before the issue was levered into the limelight with the extraordinary ministerial claim that there had been an ideological vacuum in English teaching since exam boards had scrapped formal grammar exercises. The publication of *English from 5 to 16* (1984) and the appointment of the Kingman enquiry into *The Teaching of English Language* (1987) merely provided a new twist to a familiar plot. Indeed, any account of how thinking has developed in the last 25 years has to be selective to the point of distortion. There is no lack of relevant material.

Two exchanges, one a fully fledged academic dispute, the other a more private debate within the National Association for the Teaching of English, will suffice as a way of sketching out the significant differences of opinion. In both of them, the controversy is about the relationship between 'linguistics' and 'language study'.

The publication in 1971 of *Language in Use* by Doughty, Pearce and Thornton provoked the first of these exchanges. The book included the following declaration of principle:[1]

> What pupils and students are asked to explore in language must ultimately be relatable to what Linguistic Science has to say about language. A major premise of this volume, however, is that the distance between what the specialist in Linguistic Science has to say and what is proper to work in the English class is very great.
>
> Pupils bring to the classroom a native speaker's knowledge of, and intuitions about, language and its place in human society. In this sense the task of the English teacher is not to impart a body of knowledge, but to work upon, develop, refine, and clarify the knowledge and intuitions that his pupils already possess. Consequently, he is interested in language as it affects the lives of individuals and the fabric of

society. He is unlikely to find the central concern of the specialist in linguistics, the explicit, formal and analytical description of the patterns of a language, immediately relevant to his needs.

In *Exploring Language*, published a year later, Doughty, Pearce and Thornton tackle the issue in a slightly different way by addressing the problem of whether language work undertaken in this way by teachers can still be described as 'linguistics'.

Clearly concerned that their work should remain within the general orbit of linguistics, but wishing to retain the distinction between the needs of the teacher and the concern of the specialist, they reject the idea that linguistics is concerned simply with the classification of 'elements and structures' of language and, quoting from Professor Firth, they argue for a broader definition: 'the object of linguistic analysis is to make statements of meaning so that we may see how we use language to live'.

The point they make is that the term linguistics should be taken to cover both the 'systematic and explicit analysis of the patterns of natural languages, gram- matical and phonological', *and* all other forms of 'serious and explicit intellectual enquiry into language'. This last phrase is glossed with the comment that it would cover 'the interest in language that is necessarily a part of any study of the individual or society, be it psychological, sociological or anthropological'. Under this heading comes 'Language Study' or what 'the teacher needs' to select 'from the whole range of Linguistic Studies'. An illustrative diagram might look something like Fig. 1.

The point is well illustrated in this passage from *Exploring Language*:

A great deal can be done to show how the grammatical patterns of 3- or 6- or 9-year olds differ from those of adult speakers of the language, but what must concern the

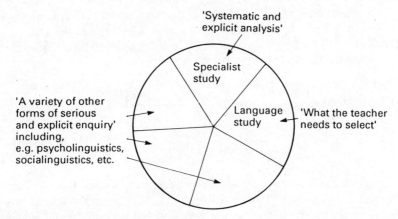

Figure 1   Linguistics

teacher is why they differ, and here the results of linguistic enquiry are likely to be tentative and suggestive rather than cut-and-dried.

What Doughty, Pearce and Thornton are claiming is that the 'specialist' will be content simply to classify the forms of the language without asking awkward questions about the significance of those forms. Theirs not to reason why. The wider questions only get asked when teachers, needing answers for Monday morning, become involved. The example provides a way of locating quite precisely the contribution of language study to linguistics, and of making the contentious point that the teachers, with their questions about 'function', are still engaged in 'linguistic enquiry'.

It has to be said, however, that the argument presents some conceptual difficulties. Doughty, Pearce and Thornton seem to be claiming language study as a branch of linguistics capable of being distinguished from other kinds of applications because of its concern with education. In making this case, however, they are betrayed by their own terminology. The term 'language study' does not sound like a branch of linguistics, rather more like an alternative definition. Equally, it has to be said that if a 'specialist' in the subject is concerned with the 'explicit formal and analytical description of the patterns of a language', then something has been conceded about how that subject works, which cannot easily be reconciled with later accounts of what is meant by 'language study'. If the specialist and the teacher are taking a different approach, then it is hard to know quite how language study qualifies as linguistics.

In *Child Language, Learning and Linguistics*, first published in 1976, David Crystal seized upon these anomalies. Under the chapter heading 'Language learning', he addresses himself, through an analysis of *Language in Use*, to the issues raised by Doughty, Pearce and Thornton (1971).

Far from being a branch of linguistics, language study, he argues, is simply a misconceived version of it in which an unwarranted emphasis has been placed on function at the expense of form. In other words, the error that Doughty, Pearce and Thompson have made is to imagine that you can talk about language by reference to what it does rather than what it is. One without the other, says Crystal, is 'sterile'. A diagram to represent Crystal's model might look something like this:

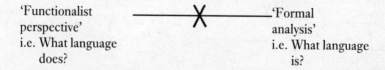

'Functionalist
perspective'
i.e. What language
    does?

'Formal
analysis'
i.e. What language
    is?

X marks the spot where it is possible to locate fruitful classroom work about language, i.e. linguistically sound, while remaining relevant to extra-linguistic educational aims. Veer too far to the right and you fall into the quicksand of traditional grammar exercises; too far to the left and you get lost in the thickets of

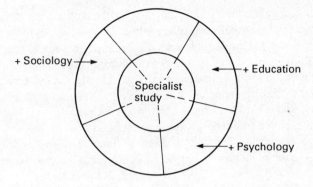

Figure 2 Linguistics

'language study'. Like Doughty *et al.*, Crystal would claim a wider definition of linguistics, but unlike them, he would argue that all those questions about 'function' are quite adequately dealt with by a single set of agreed procedures – there is no need to invent a different and ultimately competing discipline. For Crystal the only person who can answer the teacher's urgent questions is the specialist, and that is what he would wish teachers to become. If he were to redraw the diagram illustrating the approach taken by Doughty *et al.*, it might come out looking something like Fig. 2.

It is at this point that the dispute can be seen to have some bearing on important questions about what teachers and children need to know about language. What is at issue is the question of how students should be expected to talk about language. *Language in Use* claims:

> to provide an approach to the study of our own language that neither demands of the teacher specialised knowledge of Linguistic Science, nor requires of the pupil mastery of analytical procedures and unfamiliar technical terms.

David Crystal, on the other hand, writes that 'the study of English inevitably involves the imparting of some body of knowledge. I call this doing linguistics.'

In order to illustrate his case, Crystal works through a number of lessons taken from *Language in Use*. He argues that, without linguistic knowledge, teachers could be left stranded, unable to anticipate or solve the problems that arise in attempting to draw general linguistic conclusions from a mass of randomly gathered samples of language in use. The main example he provides is of a teacher investigating accent. His hypothetical lesson rapidly narrows down to a very specific point of discussion:

> If . . . the difference between north and south of England emerges over the use of /a/, as in *bath*, the point will quickly be made that the North uses short /a/ whereas the South uses long /a/. But this is only partly true as hat and calm indicate. The apparent exceptions can throw a teacher who does not expect them.

It seems a fair point, until you try and imagine the lesson in which an exchange of this kind might actually take place. 'Please, Miss, what about "hat" and "calm"?' It is not a very plausible scenario because, reasonably enough, David Crystal is thinking like a linguist and not an educationalist. Despite his strictures about function and form, he finds it hard to imagine a lesson in which the teacher is not trying to classify the forms of language. Teachers, it might reasonably be pointed out, find it hard to imagine a lesson in which they are.

The point about a lesson of this kind on accent is not to establish that there is a tendency for notherners to employ a short /a/ but, as *Language in Use* puts it, 'to examine our habit of judging an individual's personal and social history merely by listening to the way he speaks'. What Crystal fails to acknowledge, and, indeed, *Language in Use* fails to emphasize is that, for the teacher, *meaning* has to come first. Inevitably, this means committing the linguistic heresy of describing language by reference to what it does. The flaw in Crystal's argument is that he fails to provide a convincing explanation of why this is any less satisfactory than, say, describing a pair of binoculars by reference to how they change what we see, or drawing inferences about how it might have been more sensible to use a microscope.

In the early 1980s *English in Education* included a number of contributions on 'Language Study in Secondary Education' which reopened the debate. While many of the familiar arguments were rehearsed both in the initial article by Dr F. C. Stork from the Department of Linguistics at Sheffield University, and in the responses that he provoked, there were some revealing changes of emphasis that are helpful in suggesting how best to address the particular issue of language study post-16.

Despite their differences, the *Language in Use* team and David Crystal shared some common assumptions:

> A basic premise of the volume is that the development of awareness in the pupil will have a positive effect upon his competence, although this effect is likely to be indirect and may not show up immediately (Doughty *et al.*, 1971).

Indeed, Doughty *et al.* are willing to go a stage further:

> Awareness is not a vague notion at all. It is closely parallel to the kind of sensitivity towards human feelings and relationships which every teacher of English hopes to develop in his pupils through his use of literature.

It would be hard to imagine a more conventional justification of their approach. They accept without question the aims of English teaching as they were perceived at the time, claiming only that *Language in Use* will meet them more systematically than existing practice.

By arguing the value of language study for its own sake, Dr Stork makes his pitch in a quite different way. Not for him the uneasy compromise which hints at ways in which knowledge about language might improve performance, but avoids explicit claims. Maybe he enjoyed watching HMI walk into that particular trap in

English from 5 to 16 (DES, 1984). Justifications of that kind are rendered irrelevant by the simple device of drawing analogies with other subjects, and mounting a painfully partisan campaign for the allocation of curriculum space. The subject will, Dr Stork claims, 'probably teach more about how the human mind works than any other subject'. His whole edifice totters fatally on that 'probably', but he does do English teaching a good turn by reopening the question of what language study might be for, since it is on the answer to this question that we depend for any real evaluation of the 'A' level syllabuses now in operation.

In reply, Mike Torbe was unequivocal, and his article is worth quoting at some length:[2]

> What lies at the heart of this debate is not whether school pupils should or should not know more about their own language. . . . No: it is more complex, more political than that. The reasons why we want to teach our pupils about language, how it works, and its forms and functions, are not to do with 'valuable insights about language'; only a particular sort of clinical observer would want to stand back and muse on such things. We want to do it to give our pupils power over their language, and therefore over the situations in which that language is used.

What Mike Torbe does is to bypass fruitless discussions about 'performance' or 'knowledge', neither of which can adequately describe the transformations that are wrought by education. In trying to pinpoint the real value of teaching about language, Torbe accuses Dr Stork of:

> drain[ing] away from language study the real strength that it can have when it is rooted in the world that pupils live in: that is, the strength to put into our pupils' hands the ability to control their environments by giving them insights into language interactions.

This is a key point, and in what amounts to a companion piece by John Dixon (1980) in the next edition of *English in Education*, it is made again. The article, 'How to study language and the human mind?', draws attention to the 'importance [for teachers] of studying the way we use language in the classroom' and asks 'What [similar kind of enquiry] would be of equal concern for any student of 16, 17 or 18?' It is a question that both 'A' level English Language syllabuses seek to answer.

6 Language II: which syllabus?

The arrival of two Language syllabuses within a very short time of each other has inevitably provoked comparisons, and tended to polarize opinion. As a consequence, more has been made of the differences between them, than of the similarities. What is sometimes overlooked is that, on paper at least, the questions for which they are trying to find answers are the same ones. And, in their experimental phase, they have both encountered similar teething troubles.

Before going any further and leaving behind altogether the wider debate about language, it is worth being explicit about exactly what those questions are. They are listed below. As you read through, bear in mind that the answer to each question will depend, at least in part, on the answer to the question that precedes it:

1 Why study the language; for its own sake, or for what you can achieve by doing so?
2 Should language study at 'A' level be more concerned with 'function' or 'form'?
3 What place should there be for specialist linguistic terminology – a 'meta-language'?
4 Does language study demand the mastery of a 'body of knowledge' about language?
5 What place is there for the student's own skill in the language use?

It is only by being fairly tenacious in digging out answers to these questions that it is possible to get beneath the skin of either of these two syllabuses. In their respective statements about aims and objectives, for example, they neither say anything that is likely to bring the reader out in a cold sweat. The way in which principles about language study have been interpreted has to be deduced from such things as the style of the examination papers and the structure of the syllabus. It is not made explicit.

However, the syllabuses do provide a useful starting point and both are reprinted in Appendix B. For ease of reference they are represented here in a more sketchy and diagrammatic form (see Fig. 3).

	JMB		London	
40% Coursework	20% Investigation into language use 2000 – 4000 words on a chosen aspect of language use, either written or spoken		33.3% A project 3000 and transcriptions on a specific area of the spoken language based on transcription and analysis, to be assessed by the Board's examiners	**33.3% Paper 6 – The spoken language**
	20% 3 original pieces of writing 3500 – 5000 words plus a commentary. Range of writing required and drafts.			
30% Paper I	20% Critical responses to varieties of language use To describe and asses a variety of texts, both literary (10%) and non-literary (10%)		33.3% Varieties of English An examination paper providing a choice of written texts and transcripts for analysis and description. May include transcripts of speech, both literary and non-literary texts	**33.3% Paper 2 – 'Varieties'**
	10% Theoretical knowledge about the nature and functions of language (essays)			
30% Paper II	30% Interpretative uses of language A case study paper designed to assess the candidates' ability to interpret, adapt, edit and re-present given material		20% Sections 'B' and 'C' Questions based on textual material or data (10%) on particular topics (10%) designed to cover syllabus content	**33.3% Paper 5 – 'Aspects'**
			13.3% Section A An editorial task based on factual material, with a 'commentary' on the processes involved.	

Figure 3 'A' Level English Language

This kind of comparative exercise allows a number of fairly obvious points to be made. It demonstrates, for example, a clear difference of opinion about the merits of assessing the student's own use of language, JMB devoting 50 per cent of the available marks for 'Original Pieces of Writing' and 'Interpretative uses of Language'. It also highlights some differences of emphasis between the two syllabuses, in the importance attached to the spoken word, for example, or the linguistic 'content' of the exam. A chart of this kind, however, can conceal as much as it reveals. Its value is that it offers a framework for reflecting about the issues. Taken more seriously than that it can be misleading. The syllabuses themselves deserve fuller treatment.

English Language (Advanced) – JMB

It would be very tedious to launch into a lengthy account of the origins of the JMB syllabus. However, some of the early drafts of the syllabus are worth looking at for what they reveal about the intentions of the *ad hoc* working party that drew up the initial proposals. They also provide an interesting illustration of the compromises that were required by the various committees, both at the JMB and the Schools Council, whose approval was needed before the syllabus could be offered to schools.

The 'Northern Working Party' was established in response to a national conference held by the Schools Council English 16–19 project in 1978. Part of the meeting was devoted to a discussion about the possible content of an 'A' level English Language. It is quite extraordinary to reflect that, among all the different items on the shopping list, there is no mention of language study:[1]

The following elements were proposed:

1 Creative writing. There was an enthusiastic consensus that students should be encouraged to be practitioners as well as critics. During the course of the discussion the definition of 'creative writing' was broadened to include specific communication exercises, and the notion of writing for a particular audience.
2 Vocational skills. Whilst it was generally felt that the needs of industry and technology should be recognised and discussion endorsed the value of secretarial and reporting skills, reservations were expressed about the problems of assessing oral work and the blurring of the distinction between specific English work and other cross curricular skills.
3 Performance Arts. It was felt that a variety of different media should be made available for study.
4 Integration with other subjects.
5 Discriminating reading. The work of the student 'in a critical role' was still considered to be important, though it was felt that he should be encouraged to be critical about things other than lit.
6 Editorial skills. Agreement was reached on the value of this when it was defended as a means for encouraging the abilities to rework, crystallise and summarise.

What this list reveals is the instinctive cast of mind of English teachers whose academic training has left them with only one approach to language – literary criticism. While the willingness to admit some value in studying 'things other than lit.' might be judged reasonably broad minded, there is no indication that the question was even raised of whether literary criticism offered an appropriate methodology. What had attracted teachers to the meeting was the chance to continue teaching 'performance skills' beyond 16.

Put crudely, that was the breeding ground for the JMB course. It was hardly surprising, then, that the categories used in the first draft syllabus 2 years later drew attention to what candidates would be able to do, rather than what they might learn. By this time, it should be pointed out, language study had managed to force its way onto the agenda:

There are four related sections to the syllabus:
a) student as producer of language
b) student as interpreter
c) student as critic
d) student as investigator of language use.

For a number of reasons, not least of which was the division of the syllabus in four elements rather than the more conventional three, this terminology was eventually dropped. None the less, it places the course firmly in the tradition of language study recommended by Mike Torbe in *English in Education*. The four roles that it was anticipated the student would adopt put some flesh on the bones of the notion that 'we want to give our pupils power over their language, and therefore over the situations in which that language is used'. The aim was not merely that students should know more about the 'nature and functions of language' (aims) but that they should perceive language, and, therefore, reality, in a different way. 'Skills' or 'knowledge' or whatever, took second place to a proper concern with what the student could make of what they had learned.

By talking about the learner as somebody who adopts different roles, the syllabus also established a number of principles about pedagogy. It suggested, for example, that learning is an active process. That new thinking should be approached very gingerly, by experiment and hypothesis. And that *what* you do is less important than *how* you do it.

Much of this was retained, at least by implication, in the syllabus that was eventually made available as a pilot scheme. Although the proposals initially submitted to the JMB provided for a significant element of language study, they attracted criticism from the Schools Council English Committee for being insufficiently 'rigorous': 'Members tended to seek some way in which they could suggest "stiffening" the work'.[2] Cynics felt that the Committee might not be able to tell the difference between 'stiffening' and rigor mortis.

With hindsight, however, it can be conceded that there were flaws. The first syllabus submitted to the Schools Council was not specific about how literary critical techniques might be applied to 'non-literary' texts, simply assuming that it could be done. And it also failed to grasp the nettle of specifying how the 'investigation' into language would be undertaken.

The main instrument of reform was the introduction of general essay questions into the exam paper. In place of an exclusive concern with textual analysis, there was now some requirement for students to have acquired a body of linguistic knowledge. This change was a great deal more significant than might have been thought by simply adding up the number of marks (10 per cent) that were made available in the examination. The effect was felt in every nook and cranny of the syllabus. Wherever students were being expected to comment on language use, they would now do so from an explicit theoretical position.

It would be unprofitable to take this issue any further without first introducing the London syllabus, which, chronologically, was available to schools as an alternative *paper* ('Varieties of English') before the JMB syllabus had been approved. As a complete 'A' level course in English Language, however, it has only been available since 1985.

'A' Level English Language Studies – London

Again, it is useful to provide a loose historical frame for discussion of the London syllabus, since it also has evolved over a period of time. In the pilot scheme, 'Varieties of English' was provided as an alternative to the Board's 'A' English Literature literary comprehension and appreciation paper. It is partly for this reason that it is based upon textual commentary. Presumably, it was felt that only in this way could comparability with the conventional 'A' level be ensured. Interestingly, one of the earliest versions of the syllabus makes an ideological virtue out of this strategic necessity: 'The basis of the paper is that the study of literary texts should be informed by a study of other forms and uses of English.'[3] As a theoretical position it has a great deal of merit and none of the existing 'A' level literature syllabuses have a really convincing answer to this telling criticism.

Be that as it may, when the paper was submitted to the Schools Council, it received a quite different response from that accorded to the JMB syllabus. In this case, the committee felt that the theoretical base of the syllabus was *too* demanding as a further area of study in addition to the set books in the other two papers. Even in its final modified version, the syllabus is much less coy about its relationship with academic linguistics than JMB is prepared to be:

> Objectives: to demonstrate some awareness and understanding of: the nature of language variety and change; the sound and sentence patterns of present day English; factors affecting the styles and uses of English – social, regional, situational, historical; the differences between a descriptive and prescriptive attitude to language usage, and between notions of 'correct' and 'appropriate' language use; how to make a simple descriptive analysis of a text, or a contrastive analysis of two or more texts, in order to relate their linguistic features to their function and context of situation.

In their submission to the Kingman Enquiry, the Board offer the following commentary on this:

The syllabus made the linguistic frames of reference explicit, and this still looked like 'linguistics', but the aim was not a study of linguistic theory, rather an empirical investigation and description of English in use leading to some conceptual awareness of the systems of the language and an understanding of the functions of its varied forms.

While the proposers of the JMB syllabus were working their way slowly towards language study, and agonizing over the *inclusion* of a specialist terminology, the group responsible for the London syllabus was moving towards a similar position from a quite dramatically different starting point. Their problem was about what they should leave out. Where the JMB syllabus sought to answer the question 'What value might language study have for an "A" level student?', the London group had chosen to start by asking 'What version of linguistics is likely to be most appropriate for an "A" level student?'

Although the two syllabuses certainly moved some distance towards each other, it remains difficult to be certain about whether, in resolving these theoretical problems, they actually met. There ought to be a straightforward answer, but there is not.

A look at the respective examination papers and at what the syllabuses have to say about 'content' would appear to indicate that they have a great deal in common. Consider, for example, the following pairs of questions:

1(a) Explain and illustrate the importance of the distinction between formal and informal uses of languge for the study of English.

and

1(b) What interesting and important differences would a listener be likely to hear if four people were carrying on a discussion:

    (i) in a formal debate
    (ii) in an informal conversation?

Assume that the discussion was on the same topic in both situations.

Or

2(a) '"He talks like us" is equivalent to saying "He is one of us"' (Sapir, 1921). What part does language play in establishing and maintaining social groups?

and

2(b) Language habits serve to identify social groups. Show, with examples, some of the ways in which you might be able to identify which social group people belong to by listening to their speech.

If forced to guess, and each pair contains one question from each of the syllabuses, a careful reader of what has already been said about each of them might hazard that 1(a) with its slightly more abbreviated and inscrutable form of words is from the London syllabus, and that 2(b), less patently academic, is taken from a JMB paper. Neither judgement would be right, which illustrates how easy it is to stereotype the two syllabuses.[4]

It is no easier to distinguish between the two syllabuses by looking at the approach they take to the analysis of texts and transcripts. Here, for example, is the rubric from two questions designed to elicit comment on spoken English. JMB first:[5]

> The extracts which follow are from a transcription of an interview with Mr Henry Cockburn, who played football for Manchester United and England in the 1940s and 1950s.
>
> In the first extract Henry Cockburn explains how he first joined Manchester United. In the second he recalls what he was doing when he first heard about the 1958 air crash at Munich in which many of the Manchester United players were killed.
>
> The extracts are unpunctuated because they represent spoken language. HC indicates Henry Cockburn's utterances, and INT indicates the interviewer's contributions. A dash (–) stands for a pause in the flow of speech.
>
> What features of the language used in these extracts are characteristic of normal spoken English.

The second example, taken from the London paper, is also about football, though the drift of the questions is slightly different:[6]

> Here is a transcription of two broadcast commentaries of the same part of an international soccer match between England and Belgium. One is a radio commentary, the other television.
>
> Normal punctuation is not used, because this is a representation of speech, but (.) indicates a very brief pause in the commentary, and figures in brackets show the length, in seconds, of longer pauses.
>
> (i) Discuss the vocabulary concerned with sport and comment on those items which indicate that the sport is soccer, and not some other game.
> (ii) What features of the language are typical of spoken commentary, and contrast with other varieties of English (e.g. written commentary, spoken narrative etc.)?
> (iii) Explain why there are interesting differences between the radio and the television commentaries.

The resemblance between the two is uncanny, and certainly suggests that similar solutions were being devised for similar problems. In both cases, it has been thought necessary to put the extracts into context. Following that, a note has been included about the conventions adopted for describing speech, which is intended also as a broad hint to candidates that it is not acceptable to use the same terminology that they might adopt for describing written language. When, finally, the questions are reached, some differences emerge. None the less, both sets of questions are designed with the same end in mind, to encourage a discussion about the characteristics of spoken language.

A comparison of the kind of specialist linguistic knowledge considered appropriate by each syllabus is equally inconclusive, though worth persisting with, particularly since the publication of the Kingman 'model' of the English language. The similarities between all three are more striking than the differences. Each seeks to provide a broad description of how language study should be constituted. The London syllabus makes reference to:

the interrelated linguistic levels of phonology (sound pattern), or graphology (the writing system), lexis (vocabulary) and syntax (word and sentence structure) which combine to give meaning to a text or utterance in a context or situation.

The JMB put it slightly differently,

The essential elements in this area are an understanding of the nature and functions of language and a systematic study of the structure of English in terms of its phonology, grammar and semantics.

Neither are seriously at odds with the first section of the Kingman model, though it is possible to detect some differences, of more or less significance, between all three. Thus the London account is quite uncompromising in establishing a key set of categories that refer to form rather than function, thereby necessitating a rider to the effect that meaning is, of course, important. By contrast, it might be argued that although the categories employed in the JMB syllabus are roughly similar, the reference to 'semantics' makes meaning a more central part of the enterprise. The Kingman 'model' employs a rather different organizing principle, preferring to categorize units of language according to their length (see Fig. 4).

Given the purpose for which this model is primarily intended, the greater understanding of children's language use, it is an odd choice. The 'logic' that insists on a 'model' being built up from individual units (words) is not likely to offer teachers much insight into their pupils' actual use of language, being so remote from any cultural or social understandings about how language works. None the less, within these broad frameworks, much the same ground is covered.

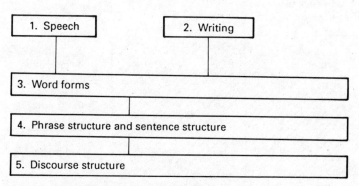

Figure 4 The forms of the English language.

All three models seek to say something further than this about the way in which language works. In the examination syllabuses, these tend to emerge as 'topics' or 'objectives'; in the Kingman report, they are simply further 'parts' of the whole. Figure 5 which attempts to summarize the differences between the three is crude, but suggestive.

Two points are worth making. The first is that the London syllabus is light on language acquisition. In so far as the whole cast of the syllabus suggests an unwillingness to take account of the candidates' own language development, this might be thought predictable. It does provide a hint, though, of some kind of difference between the two syllabuses that is not merely cosmetic. They both have more in common with each other, however, than they do with the Kingman model, which pointedly replaces the concept of a social dimension to language, with the much more limited notion of 'Communication' and 'Comprehension'. Although both approaches are designed to acknowledge something about the 'context' within which language is used, there is a real difference between them. A social or cultural view acknowledges that language emerges out of the complex experience of the person using it, and must be shaped according to their perceptions and needs. The recommendations in Kingman are for something much thinner than this, something that is much more about how users of

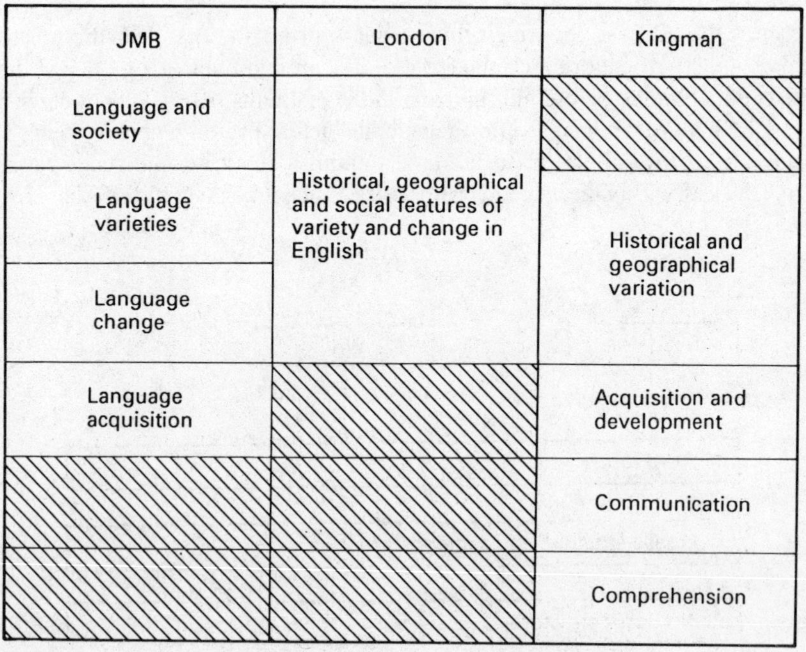

JMB	London	Kingman
Language and society	Historical, geographical and social features of variety and change in English	///
Language varieties		Historical and geographical variation
Language change		
Language acquisition	///	Acquisition and development
///	///	Communication
///	///	Comprehension

Figure 5   Differences between the JMB, London and Kingman models.

language must conform to the linguistic demands of the situation in which they find themselves. It denies their rights over language.

Given the apparent similarities between the two 'A' level syllabuses, similarities which are highlighted by the comparison with Kingman, it is curious that the Chief Examiner for the London Board should have remarked in the *Times Educational Supplement* that:

> they [the JMB proposals] failed to appreciate the need, at that level, of the controlling and informing content of an academic discipline. For the study of literature this is literary criticism; for the study of language, it is linguistics.

It is an interesting judgement, which prompts the suspicion that there must be some important differences between the two syllabuses that this comparison has not yet brought to light. The simple equation of 'A' level syllabuses and academic disciplines is particularly suggestive. It helps to explain some of the decisions that were taken when the 'Varieties of English' paper was developed into a complete examination. Two features of 'English Language Studies' warrant further attention. The first of these is the stipulation that the project must be an investigation of the *spoken* language, the second is the inclusion of an 'editorial task'.

The project first. The significance attached to it is made explicit in the Board's response to the Kingman Enquiry, which, in its outline of the syllabus, points out that 'spoken language is fundamental to knowledge about language'. There is nothing particularly controversial about this view among linguists. Most standard introductions to the subject make the same point. Here, for example, is J. F. Wallwork (1969) in *Language and Linguistics*:

> Most linguists now prefer to study the spoken forms of the language, basing their decision to do so on good grounds. They argue that the oral approach is justified, firstly, by the fact that historically it is evident that speech must have preceded writing. . . . If one wishes to study language, it is logical to go to the primary source, i.e. spoken language, rather than the derived secondary source, such as writing represents.

Without having been privy to the discussions that took place, it is impossible to know whether the emphasis on the spoken language grew out of educational priorities or the desire for linguistic orthodoxy. Given the Board's evidence to Kingman on this point, it seems reasonable to assume the latter.

The second significant addition to the syllabus was the inclusion of an editorial task, which invites comparison with the JMB 'Case Study'. What follows is taken directly from the specimen papers produced prior to the first examination:

> The extract below is from a road craft manual published by Her Majesty's Stationery Office in 1955.

> (i) Rewrite the paragraphs in language that you think would be appropriate in a similar booklet for today's reader, and

(ii) comment and explain how your choice of language differs from that of the original.

1. One of the most difficult problems which beset the night driver is found in built up areas where the street lighting is inferior. Frequently he finds that his view consists alternately of pools of light from street lamps, and of darkness where the street lighting fails to penetrate owing to lack of power or to obstruction by overhanging trees. He is advised to illuminate these pools of darkness by using his headlamps whenever he can do so without danger to other road users. Frequently, of course, this will be impossible owing to approaching traffic, and in this event he should drive on his dipped headlamps or pass-lamp at a speed suited to the conditions. It is dangerous to black out completely by driving on side lamps only.

2. The driver will find that, whilst his own lights illuminate many objects on the road, he will see a great deal from the lights of other vehicles, particularly those approaching. The glare of the headlights of traffic approaching round bends or coming along converging roads gives ample warning of approach and also a guide to the severity of bends and corners. Objects on the road ahead often appear as silhouettes in the approaching lights.

3. Night driving is always a severe test of endurance. A driver should prepare himself by taking sufficient rest beforehand. Fatigue will first be felt as eyestrain, for continuous looking along a beam of light is most tiring. If drowsiness overtakes him, he should not try to overcome it whilst still driving; he should stop, 'have a stretch', rest his eyes for a little while, and have a drink of hot tea or coffee. Any change from driving will restore the failing power of concentration and observation.

In common with much of the rest of the paper, it is a cunningly constructed task, which unobtrusively demands a close focus on the text, and leaves candidates in no doubt about what they are doing. However, lingering doubts remain about whether the question is really designed to 'assess their [the candidates] own writing' as the syllabus claims. The writer has little scope for making any significant decisions about the piece and it is difficult to see how the finished product can have any real value in its own right. What distinguishes this task from others on the exam papers is that it implies a different *pedagogic* approach. While this is a perfectly worthy, and worthwhile ambition, the skills being assessed remain essentially the same as in the rest of the syllabus, as the second part of the question makes clear – 'comment and explain'. The main purpose of the editorial task is to prompt observations about language change.

It is for this reason that the London syllabus is far less vulnerable to the charge, which has been levelled at the JMB syllabus, of being a 'hybrid'. The JMB 'Case Study' quite brazenly sets out to test all manner of things that have a much less direct relationship with linguistic study. The specimen paper, for example, included an assignment based on the poems and letters of Wilfred Owen. The version reproduced here has been abbreviated (see Fig. 6), though the task remains as it was in the original:

The letters in Folder B1 were written by Wilfred Owen and sent to his mother (Susan Owen) between 1st. January 1917 and 4th. February 1917. They describe his arrival in France on the way to the front, and his first experience of being under fire during the battle of the Somme. On page 7 you will find two poems written by Owen soon after – 'The Show' and 'The Sentry'.

Task:

You have been asked by the BBC (radio 4) to provide a short radio programme about this period in Wilfred Owen's life and his first experience of the war in France. You may, of course, use extracts from the letter and poems if you wish, but your script should not be composed entirely of Owen's own words since a selection of readings from the letters (without commentary) has recently been broadcast on the same channel and your producer is looking for a different approach.

There is no mistaking the untidy way in which this spills over into all kinds of other curriculum areas. While it quite explicitly makes demands on the student's ability to understand and produce a text, it also implies some familiarity with literary criticism for discussion of the two poems, and media education for an adequate understanding of the proposed audience. The written task has a stated function which, even though it is simulated, establishes the credibility of the writer and bears out the aim of the syllabus to 'combine learning about the nature and function of language in human thought and communication with learning how to use English more effectively'.

It is probably fair to say that these differences are more important than they may seem to be. A simple audit of the two syllabuses such as that represented by Fig. 4 implies no more than that the two exam boards had different shopping lists. What it misses is a sense of what happens when all the ingredients are combined.

Nowhere is this more evident than in the approach that each syllabus adopts towards the issue of specific linguistic terminology. For anybody wanting to make straightforward comparisons, there are frustrations. While the London syllabus provides a 'selected list of terms as a guide', JMB maintains a studied silence. It is possible to interpret this as an indication that the syllabus lacks confidence about its own proposed methodology, or to see it as a baffling failure to support teachers struggling with a new discipline. The issue, however, is not quite that straightforward. Some understanding of why the JMB syllabus is so circumspect is provided by the 1986 Examiner's report. Running through the text of the report is a preoccupation with questions about why some answers are better than others. Here is a selection of comments extracted from different sections of the report:[7]

Candidates whose metalanguage did not go beyond conventional names for parts of speech found themselves making such statements as: 'There are no verbs at the two-word stage' and 'By three years old a child can manage simple conjunctions like "and" and "but"' ('simple' was not underlined in the script). At its extreme end this perspective produced the thesis that 'a child's utterances are frequently grammatically incorrect,' a surprisingly common assumption, and one which more often closed than opened discussion.

How far identification went depended largely on candidates' theoretical frameworks and on their willingness to develop general or subjective judgements.

Figure 6 Extract from material provided for JMB case study 'Wilfred Owen'.

475. To Susan Owen

1 January 1917   *[France]*

This is a sort of Hotel Camp where none stay more than 2 or 3 days!

I have not been uncomfortable so far, with a tent to myself, and with a diligent Orderly.

This morning I was hit! We were bombing and a fragment from somewhere hit my thumb knuckle. I coaxed out 1 drop of blood. Alas! no more!!

There is a fine heroic feeling about being in France, and I am in perfect spirits. A tinge of excitement is about me, but excitement is always necessary to my happiness.

480. To Susan Owen

Tues: 16 January 1917   *[2nd Manchester Regt., B.E.F.]*

Three quarters dead, I mean each of us ¾ dead, we reached the dug-out, and relieved the wretches therein. I then had to go forth and find another dug-out for a still more advanced post where I left 18 bombers. I was responsible for other posts on the left but there was a junior officer in charge.

My dug-out held 25 men tight packed. Water filled it to a depth of 1 or 2 feet, leaving say 4 feet of air.

One entrance had been blown in & blocked.

So far, the other remained.

The Germans knew we were staying there and decided we shouldn't.

Those fifty hours were the agony of my happy life.

Every ten minutes on Sunday afternoon seemed an hour.

I nearly broke down and let myself drown in the water that was now slowly rising over my knees.

Towards 6 o'clock, when, I suppose, you would be going to church, the shelling grew less intense and less accurate: so that I was mercifully helped to do my duty and crawl, wade, climb and flounder over No Man's Land to visit my other post. It took me half an hour to move about 150 yards.

I was chiefly annoyed by our own machine guns from behind. The seeng-seeng-seeng of the bullets reminded me of Mary's canary. On the whole I can support the canary better.

481. To Susan Owen

Friday, 19 January 1917   [*2nd Manchester Regt., B.E.F.*]

They want to call No Man's Land 'England' because we keep supremacy there.

It is like the eternal place of gnashing of teeth; the Slough of Despond could be contained in one of its crater-holes; the fires of Sodom and Gomorrah could not light a candle to it – to find the way to Babylon the Fallen.

It is pock-marked like a body of foulest disease and its odour is the breath of cancer.

I have not seen any dead. I have done worse. In the dank air I have <u>perceived</u> it, and in the darkness, <u>felt</u>. Those 'Somme Pictures' are the laughing stock of the army – like the trenches on exhibition in Kensington.

No Man's Land under snow is like the face of the moon chaotic, crater-ridden, uninhabitable, awful, the abode of madness.

482. To Susan Owen

Sunday, 4 February 1917   [*Advanced Horse Transport Depot*]

The marvel is that we did not all die of cold. As a matter of fact, only one of my party actually froze to death before he could be got back, but I am not able to tell how many have ended in hospital. I had no real casualties from shelling, though for 10 minutes every hour whizz-bangs fell a few yards short of us. Showers of soil rained on us, but no fragments of shell could find us.

I had lost my gloves in a dug-out, but I found 1 mitten on the Field; I had my Trench Coat (without lining but with a Jerkin underneath). My feet ached until they could ache no more, and so they temporarily died. I was kept warm by the ardour of Life within me. I forgot hunger in the hunger for Life. The intensity of your Love reached me and kept me living. I thought of you and Mary without a break all the time. I cannot say I felt any fear. We were all half-crazed by the buffetting of the High Explosives. I think the most unpleasant reflection that weighed on me was the impossibility of getting back any wounded, a total impossibility all day, and frightfully difficult by night.

We were marooned on a frozen desert.

There is not a sign of life on the horizon and a thousand signs of death.

Not a blade of grass, not an insect; once or twice a day the shadow of big hawk, scenting carrion.

The type of explanation generally reflected the theoretical frameworks available to candidates.

A distinction is being drawn between the acquisition of a 'theoretical framework' which will help candidates develop a more sophisticated view of language, and the use of a specialist vocabulary which may prove inhibiting. Terminology is not what matters.

This, of course, leaves teachers with some difficult judgements to make. The most important of these is about how to study language in a way that is both systematic and exploratory. While there is no single solution to this problem, it is fairly easy to recognize what has happened when the teacher has got it right. Consider, for example, the way in which Peter Stockwell, a student at St Mary's Sixth Form College in Middlesbrough, writes about a short story that he had submitted as one of his three pieces of original writing. The full text of *Tom's Last Voyage* is reproduced in Appendix A at the end of this book and is worth reading for its own sake. The story is a dramatic monologue in which Tom, who is finally admitted to an old people's home, gradually loses touch with reality as his mental condition deteriorates. Here is the 'commentary' required by the JMB syllabus:

Tom's Last Voyage (3000 words)

This piece is in the form of a dramatic monologue, narrated in the first person. The style is obviously conversational which can be seen in the frequent use of the following devices.

The most obvious devices are colloquialisms, clichés and swearwords. These swearwords, which are spread liberally throughout the story, increase in frequency and obscenity as Tom becomes angry. For instance, he moves from the relatively mild, 'buggers,' and, 'bloody past admirers,' in the beginning to the stronger, 'Middle of the afternoon my arse!' and, 'Bitches!' in moments of anger.

Throughout, he uses simple vocabulary which takes on an almost childlike simplicity towards the end as his mind degenerates:

'The people here are nice,' and, 'As soon as that's done we'll be off!'

Tom contracts his words, as in speech: 'I've,' 'There's,' and so on, and his sentences themselves are often short, sharp and grammatically 'incorrect' as in:

'Still. I could've settled down. Family? None as such,' and, 'I didn't think it were possible.' Often he adds summarising statements to these, as headlines or after-thoughts:

'There were some next door. Young folk, that is,' and he corrects himself or modifies an idea:

'Oh, a sister . . . Alice, in Brazil, or somewhere,' and, '. . . could have been my daughter, grand-daughter!' These uncertainties, corrections and downright contra-dictions increase in frequency as the story progresses, showing Tom's degenerating and confused mind:

'I . . . must have knocked a cup. . . . Maybe it was her dropped the cup. . . . I think I was angry with her then, for breaking the cup.'

His wandering mind is also revealed in his digression in his subject matter. Tom rambles, often straying from the point – 'That's your old decrepit mind wandering again.'

He often repeats himself too:

'Two of them. Clever. Can't watch two of them . . . Clever.' He uses exclamations – 'Oh God!' and there is a lack of imperatives. Where they are used, they are softened:

'Oh, don't get me wrong.' Tom also, appropriately, and as in speech, has a habit of storytelling, beginning paragraphs with, 'One day,' or, 'One evening,' or, 'One afternoon.'

Tom often uses direct speech, when describing his conversations with the social workers or the children. From time to time he incorporates someone else's speech into his own narrative:

'Make yourself comfortable. This is your home.' This becomes more and more frequent, until Tom reaches the point where his awareness of reality becomes dream-like, and he incorporates the speech of the girl's mother in a flood of reported words:

'. . . shouldn't I know better than that what the hell did I think I was doing?' This, combined with the lack of punctuation in this paragraph, gives an effect of flooding words striking Tom; and the parallel with the rain is made explicit:

'. . . the rain trickling down her flattened hair and the words streaming out of her mouth.' 'Streaming' is a stronger word than 'trickling' and this gives the impression that the woman outdoes the downpour with her words.

This difference that Tom creates between his own speech in narrative and that of the other characters serves to reflect his isolation. Outside himself are 'Them – the Social Services.' All the other main characters are women. Tom 'didn't understand women – all they meant to me was a thing during shore-leave.' So, as objects to him, their speech is different. Anna, the social worker, for example, speaks to him patronisingly, 'sing-song,' 'like a naughty boy:'

'Here it is, all found!'

As his mind degenerates, his narrative paragraphs become longer, with less and less order in the form of punctuation, and more and more repetition:

'. . . it didn't really matter it was just like a calm day somewhere near the equator, or just to the south, except, of course, that the sea was grey and not blue and the horizon stayed still and there were clouds in the sky but it didn't matter, it didn't matter at all . . .'

This degeneration is also illustrated in the fact that he addresses himself more and more as he continues, also showing his isolation – 'Tom, my old son.'

The reader has to deduce the real facts of Tom's senility from these variations in style, since Tom does not have the capability to recognise it any more. Thus there are two versions of the story: the one Tom tells in which he ends in a ship; and the one the reader deduces of Tom in an old people's home.

On page six the narrative moves into the present tense ('The people here are nice') to show that Tom has been telling the story from the home. Thus, perhaps, it is unlikely that his mind would be as clear at the beginning of the story as it is; however, I needed the past tense to enable me to move through months quickly without describing every detail. The change in tense has the additional advantage of pointing a contrast between Tom's past awareness and his present unawareness, symbolised by his burning of his own photo.

The final sentence ('Don't let the buggers put you down!') is a variation of a similar sentence at the beginning ('Don't let the buggers push you under') which lends a sense of unity to the story and also rounds it off nicely with an exclamation of a defiant spirit, which prevents the essentially sad story becoming too demoralising. Although Tom's mind has gone, we know he is happy.

There is some evidence here that linguistic terminology has been acquired – 'colloquialism . . . cliché . . . exclamations . . . imperatives . . . tense . . .', and so on – but that is probably the least important feature of the commentary. Much more interesting is the frame of reference that Peter Stockwell has used to comment, with quite remarkable perception, on his own work. Throughout he draws attention to the significance of different kinds of language use, starting with the observation that the piece is in the form of a 'dramatic monologue', and that the style is 'obviously conversational'. Further on, he makes reference to 'story-telling', 'direct speech', 'narrative' and 'reported words', all of which have a key role to play in representing something about Tom's state of mind. What makes the work impressive, is the confidence with which the student both handles and comments on language variety – a concept which needs to be right at the centre of the English curriculum.

There is one other point that is worth making about this approach to language study. The choice of a piece of original writing as an illustration was deliberate. It allows a link to be established between the content of the syllabus and the way in which it is taught. Put more simply, it illustrates the way in which language acquisition and learning is the same for 18-year-olds as for 2-year-olds. The process does not, at some fixed point in a person's life, cease to be dynamic and cognitive. There is no stage at which anybody can simply be *told* how language works. One of the values of encouraging students to continue to develop their own use of language is that it provides the most effective means there is to reflect about language and acts as a corrective to assembly line theories that treat language as if it were merely a matter of predictable linguistic responses, more or less successfully related to context.

7 Language III: language and literature

Both syllabuses also had to confront the major problem of how language and literature relate to each other. The conceptual difficulties (for linguists) of sorting out an answer based on satisfactory categories of language, were compounded by the reality of 'A' level English Literature with its monopoly control over the post-16 curriculum.

The position that the JMB syllabus adopts is characteristically pragmatic. Without providing any justification for doing so, other than the instinctive feeling that it is a special kind of language use, the syllabus reserves a whole section within Paper 1 for critical response to literature. By contrast, the London Board clearly wrestled with its conscience before making the rather grudging pledge that *Varieties of English* 'might include transcripts of speech and extracts from both literary and non-literary texts'. As if to excuse itself from all responsibility for such a transgression of the linguistic proprieties, the Board offers the following alibi to the Kingman Enquiry:

> The inclusion of 'literary' passages had been at the request of the Schools Council and the Secondary Examinations Council in approving the syllabuses. There was no theoretical distinction between the language of 'literary' and 'non-literary', though literary texts might be characterised by specific literary forms, such as the sonnet or the short story, and there could be major distinctions in the contextual roles of writer and reader.

In spite of the difficulties that both syllabuses experienced in reconciling language and literature, the significance of the attempt should not be underestimated. In judging what language study has to offer literary criticism, it is easy to get waylaid by debates about stylistics. There are other issues that have much greater implications for the construction of syllabuses for 16- to 19-year-olds.

It is quite helpful to start by looking at the kind of questions that Language Study might ask about a text (taken from the London Board *Varieties of English* paper):[1]

What features of the language are typical of . . .
Say which varieties of English you think they represent . . .
Discuss how far the language of the primers resembles real speech . . .
How can we recognise the difference between . . .
Identify these deviations from . . .

What all these questions do, of course, is to place the language in a wider context, and by doing so draw attention to the ways in which meaning is socially constructed. Suddenly, and because these are the questions that conventional syllabuses do not ask, literary studies begin to look a little isolated. No 'A' level English Literature student is asked to think about what literature is, about how the language used to construct meaning in literature derives its own meaning from other kinds of use, or about how such language might be read. And there is nothing particularly problematic about asking those questions. There is no need for a vocabulary that is any more specialist than is currently required for 'A' level literature.

This point needs to be worked through in some detail if it is to be firmly established. In attempting to do this, I have chosen to quote at some length from the opening chapter of *Benefits* by Zoe Fairbairns (1979), a book unlikely to be selected as a prescribed text for a conventional syllabus. I make some apologies for the length of the extract, but would argue that it is necessary given the nature of the exercise. It is difficult to look at the way in which different *types* of language operate in literature without allowing them to become fully established in the text:

1

Summer of Seventy-Six

It was a tall, wide structure, and it stood like a pack of chewing gum, upended in a grudging square of grass on the side of a hill. It was made of glass, grey metal and rough brown brick, and had a depressing but all-too-familiar history. It was one of the last tower blocks to be built in the sixties for London families to live in. By the time it was up, planners, builders and social workers were already losing faith in tower blocks and the families that moved in from the dirty, neighbourly streets being cleared around Collindeane's feet did so without enthusiasm.

Ninety-six flats had meant more than twice that many children; but once the older boys had staked territorial claims to the grass patch, no one young or weak got a look-in. The boys found other sources of fun: filling the lift with bricks, tying door-knockers together, calling in the fire-brigade. Windows got smashed. Families withheld rent and were evicted; or vanished overnight, leaving massive arrears and furniture that had not been paid for. Childish high spirits turned malignant. Paraffin was poured through letterboxes and lit; human shit was left on landings; bricks and planks and crockery were thrown from high windows. Soon anyone with any choice in the matter moved out of the flats, leaving behind only those with no choice. Teenage mothers who looked forty. Drunken, shuffling, unemployed men. Ragged litters of children, yelling as they slithered down the endless banisters or hung from high windows to terrorise passers-by. Old folk with multiple locks on the doors, peering out at the stray dogs that met and fought and mated in the corridors.

Disease entered the flats – pneumonia, gastroenteritis, rumours of typhoid, even a rabies scare – and the council said it would close the flats and pull them down. The local paper declared such waste inexcusable. The council promised to rehabilitate instead, and put up some swings. But before this could be done, the curtain came down on the era of affluence that had spawned and nurtured the British welfare state. The international oil crisis brought inflation that galloped through dreams, slashed welfare budgets. There was no money to rehabilitate Collindeane Tower. The council closed it, rehoused its inmates, nailed wooden planks across the doorway and tried to pretend they had never built it, indeed had not noticed it was there – one of the biggest, most embarrassing statutory nuisances on the London skyline.

Soon after, Collindeane Tower was spotted by a group of women looking for somewhere to squat and establish a feminist community. One of them chopped through the planks with her axe, and they moved in while the council averted its eyes.

Everyone who was in London in the summer of 1976 remembers the weather. The four-month heatwave brought pleasure at first, then incredulity, then resignation and unease as the curious realities of urban drought upset the jocular complacency of those who would never have believed that Londoners would pray for rain. People remember what they were doing that summer in the same way that they can pinpoint their location and activity at the time they heard about the death of President Kennedy.

From May to September, misty mornings preceded glaring debilitating days and dry airless nights. The Thames became unnavigable. Workers went on strike for better ventilation. Grass browned, trees drooped, earth subsided under foundations and buildings cracked. Commuters left jackets and cotton cardigans at home and adhered to each other in packed trains, licking ices. Umbrella sellers went out of business, shorts were worn in the staidest of offices, and members of parliament were outraged by the price of cold drinks in Oxford Street. Day followed incredible day and still the heat did not let up, still it did not rain. Once or twice a grey, brooding constipated sky rumbled and flashed and a few drops of water fell, but you could not call that rain; not when there was talk of standpipes in the streets and even Buckingham Palace (it was rumoured) had a sign up in the loo saying 'Don't pull for a pee.' It rained enough, it was true, to kill the Saturday of the Lord's Test against Australia (if it had to rain one day of the year, Londoners told each other wisely, that would be the one) but that was not enough to break the drought – an almost indecent word to be used about their city, thought Londoners, to whom drought meant sandy deserts and cracked farmland in places near the equator. In unaccustomed chats between strangers, sympathy for our own farmers (pictured each night on television running dust through their fingers and waving parched roots as if the government ought to do something about it) alternated only with contrived sighs of ecstasy: 'Isn't it glorious?'. Londoners did not really believe in farmers.

Women active in what was then known as the women's liberation movement have other reasons for remembering that summer. One of the major demands of that movement was for a woman's right to abortion on demand. It seemed axiomatic that women could not advance without full control of their fertility; and as things stood, abortion was only allowed when a woman was ill enough, or stressed enough, or rich enough to persuade two doctors ('acting in good faith' the law insisted), to say it would be good for her. And throughout that summer, a Select Committee of MPs, under pressure from organised anti-feminists, was considering ways of making abortions even more difficult to obtain, particularly for those women who sought them merely because they did not wish to be pregnant. The women's liberationists' response to these efforts was to commit themselves, this gleaming summer, to vigorous grassroots campaigning; marches, pickets, petitions, letter-writing, all aimed at showing that parliament (which appeared to have an anti-abortion majority) was out of step with the public on this issue.

The women were interested in another parliamentary fight too: the 'child benefits' issue. The government of the day had a longstanding commitment to making a weekly cash payment to mothers, financing this by increased taxation of fathers; transferring money, as the newspapers liked coyly to put it, 'from wallet to purse'. Unfortunately, at just the time when this scheme was due to come into effect, the government was making a deal with the mighty trade union movement (mighty compared with the organised strength of mothers) that the workers would reduce their pay-demands if the government would reduce taxation. Stalemate. The government had made two contradictory promises, one to women and one to trade unionists, mainly men; and so it was, late in May, that the government flew in the face of its commitment to women's rights and postponed the child benefit scheme indefinitely.

Feminist anger and agitation about this was less vocal and coherent, however, than the response to the Select Committee's threat to abortion rights. Abortion was a simple matter. Anyone who did not approve of abortion did not have to have one, but it should be each individual woman's right to choose. Child benefits, though – that raised other issues. Of course it was monstrous that the organised males of the trade union movement should object to their wives having a right to some of 'their' money, monstrous that sexism should so blatantly coerce government policy. But feminists weren't sure that they wanted men's miserable paypackets docked to finance child benefits, they weren't sure they wanted to be paid to stay at home and have children, which was how some of them saw it. Shortly after the government announced its decision, a gathering of women sat and argued these points on the roof of Collindeane Tower.

Lynn Byers was thirty-two, short, red-haired and a journalist; she freelanced occasionally for the local paper and had been a vitriolic opponent of the demolition of Collindeane, though privately she had known that all the rehabilitation in the world would not make a 24-storey tower suitable for children to live in. Lynn lived with her husband Derek in a house that they had bought for a song in nearby Seyer Street. The house was cheap partly because it was falling down and partly because Seyer Street was a slum; but it was harmless enough for a healthy couple in their thirties, for whom freedom from a heavy mortgage far outweighed the odd rat.

Lynn had never been in a women's liberation group, though she had felt complete sympathy with the movement insofar as she perceived it from *Spare Rib* and the women's page in the *Guardian*. She'd been on a few marches, usually alone, and was as incensed as anyone about child benefits and the threat to abortion rights. She was in a state of ambivalence herself about having children – the steady advance of the years, Derek's clearly stated (but not harped upon) desire for fatherhood, and her own curiosity and yearning vied with the knowledge of how hard it would be to give up the independence and pride of self-employment and self-support. And political events weighed heavily against having children. The mammoth arrogance of a government closing off women's escape route from unwanted pregnancy while at the same time withholding the tiny improvement that they'd promised in mothers' financial position, made Lynn sweat with rage.

The women in the tower had been friendly enough to Lynn, particularly in the early days of their occupancy when the weather was still cold and she brought them thermoses of coffee and let them use her bath and her phone; but she never felt fully accepted, partly, she supposed, because she was married and liked her husband (quite apart from loving him); and partly because she earned her living. She had no particular objections to people squatting or drawing social security, which was how most of the women lived, or, for that matter, to the one called Marsha living on money inherited from a dead relative, most of which she had paid into an account to which all the women had access for the refurbishment of the flats. It seemed a perfectly reasonable use for state or private wealth. Nevertheless, Lynn had the feeling that they had the feeling that she disapproved. Or perhaps it was just Marsha. Marsha was new to the group, and, despite having been the one who struck the first blow to the planks boarding up Collindeane with her axe, didn't actually live there. This was partly (she admitted to Lynn one day when no one was listening, obviously seeing her as a partner in the crime of *incomplete commitment*) because she liked to escape to her own place, and partly because she had a boyfriend called David who was a social worker of rather traditional opinions who would not visit her in a women's commune even if he were allowed through the door. Marsha compensated for her assorted guilts by recounting, to anyone who would listen, conversations in which she had rebuked David for his authoritarian and moralistic attitude to his clients, twiddling her long, dark hair, and pouring her money and energy into the flats. In fact, Lynn doubted how far the thing would have got without her; many of the other twenty-odd women seemed to prefer consciousness-raising to clearing out rubble.

A conventional literary critical approach might start by drawing attention to the structure of the passage. The book opens with a visual description of Collingdeane Tower which, despite being reinforced by an explanation of its immediate past history, remains essentially specific and concrete. It is only at the very end of this section that the first event of some significance for the subsequent narrative is mentioned. And it is immediately forgotten in favour of the even broader, and more anonymous, perspective provided in the next two sections which sketch in, respectively, the literal and the intellectual climate of the time. This panoramic survey is held together by a second reference, at the end of the third section, to the narrative, which is used to prepare the reader for the introduction of Lynn Byers, the first 'character' to warrant a mention. The description of her that follows, then, can only be read within the quite specific framework of what has preceded it.

Literary criticism might offer a number of ways of describing what is happening here. At 'A' level, it is likely that there would be much talk of the move from the general towards the specific, and of the way in which the author has prepared us for a novel of ideas. We have been softened up, as it were, for the polemic, and it is quite clear that individual characters are going to take second place.

An 'A' level class might go on to look in some detail at the way in which the language is used and begin to register points that could refer forward to what happens in the rest of the novel. Conscious, because the structure has already been mapped out in some detail, that the novel is about women, and that the author is clearly interested in feminism, it is likely that the tower itself would be identified as a phallic symbol. The invasion of the tower by the women who squat in it, clearly signifies the triumph of feminism over patriarchal masculinity. The fate of the tower will later turn out to reflect the fate not just of the protagonists but of all women. Literary criticism is beginning to provide insights that allow us to see the text as multilayered, and to suggest a resonance in the language that is unique to literature.

The polemic is further reinforced by the direct, evocative descriptions of place. In the second paragraph, for example, the vandalism is ascribed to 'the older *boys*', while children roam the area in 'litters', their mothers, the women, being ascribed no more status than animals. It is only those who are actually old and those who seem old either because of unemployment ('shuffling men') or pregnancy ('teenage mothers who looked forty') that remain. The imaginative world that Zoe Fairbairns has created leaves us in no doubt who are the oppressed, and who the oppressors.

The other significant frame that is created in these opening paragraphs is of the sterility of urban life – 'Londoners did not really believe in farmers'. In the heat, nothing will grow. The feeling is apocalyptic, earth subsides and buildings crack. This, you are meant to feel, is the achievement of the male, corporate state. Throughout the book, an ironic contrast is sustained with the fertility of women, itself so difficult to control.

What this analysis has tended to do is to stress the imaginative unity of the book. While drawing attention to the skill of the writer as an artist, it ironically deflects attention from what she is actually saying. We are too busy labelling, docketing, evaluating and admiring to listen.

An alternative approach, which depends upon being allowed to illuminate the text with insights culled from language study, places the stress elsewhere. It also provides a tentative explanation of why the literary term that causes most problems at 'A' level is 'tone'. Almost all students experience difficulty with the term – many find it impossible to detect anything at all to which it might refer. And yet it is only possible to talk about literature without mentioning tone by ignoring much that is most subtle and revealing about the meaning of a work. It is a difficult idea because it implies some understanding of language variety, and, as a consequence, is unlikely to be acquired through reading eight set works of literature.

Looked at like this, the opening pages of *Benefits* can be read in a different, though complementary, way. The text becomes a weave of different types of language.

One important role that Zoe Fairbairns adopts is that of social historian:

> Women active in what was then known as the women's liberation movement have other reasons for remembering that summer. One of the major demands of that movement was for a woman's right to abortion on demand.

Two phrases – 'what was then known' and 'that movement' – serve to distance the writer from her material and suggest a clinical detachment. Indeed, the device of referring to 'Women active . . .' implicitly denies any commitment on the part of the narrator. This Olympian tone is sustained by the calculated use of dates to provide a sense that what is being surveyed is the broad sweep of history – 'the last tower block built in the sixties', 'the summer of 1976', 'From May to September', and so on. Judicious reference to familiar public events – the Lord's Test, for example – reinforces the sense of documentary truth.

The second voice, like the first, belongs to the narrator. It is the voice of the pamphleteer, the polemicist. Its stock in trade, like a certain kind of politician, is heavy rhetorical ironies:

> as things stood, abortion was only allowed when a woman was ill enough, or stressed enough, or rich enough to persuade two doctors ('acting in good faith' the law insisted) to say it would be good for her. And throughout that summer a Select Committee of MPs, under pressure from organised anti-feminists, was considering ways of making abortions even more difficult to obtain, particularly for those women who sought them merely because they did not wish to be pregnant.

The third voice that speaks in these opening pages is Lynn Byers, as reported in Zoe Fairbairns' account of her. It is the voice of a querulous, intelligent woman as she might *speak* to us, and characteristically it reserves the right to dissent from received opinion. It is the voice of the middle class defending itself against ideology. Lynn was '*as incensed as anyone* about child benefits', she 'liked her husband (*quite apart from loving him*)', and she had '*had no particular objection* to people squatting'. There are two ways in which 'A' level students might become attuned to that voice. One is to read a great deal, the other is to be encouraged to think about, and become aware of, language variety. It tells the reader more about Lynn Byers than almost anything else in the passage, and it helps to pinpoint some of the unresolved problems of the novel.

The relationship between these three voices is a complex one. In making sense of it, it is helpful if the reader has some notions about how these different kinds of language work. The language of historical reconstruction is one of generalization and selection. The skill of the social historian lies in the ability to capture the significant characteristics of a particular passage of time. Zoe Fairbairns does this with some skill – 'By the time it was up, planners, builders and social workers were already losing faith in tower blocks . . .'. The language is used to insist that that is how it was. The aim is to ward off alternative interpretations. Indeed, she refuses to admit that it is an 'interpretation' at all. In this version of events, society is characterized as a kind of constantly evolving consensus far removed from the antics of any individual action or belief.

The second voice, that of fierce commitment, contrasts sharply with the first, and the way in which Zoe Fairbairns slides from one to the other is sometimes quite disorientating, as, no doubt, it is meant to be. It employs a language of extremes, that works through reiteration and rhetoric. It is a speaking voice, but of a very public kind, whose aim is to provoke disagreement, to be divisive, to represent reality as a mosaic of warring factions. History, in this version, is composed of individuals who change the way the world is.

The language that Lynn Byers uses is different again. All of her (assumed) utterances actually defy the orthodox view, whatever that may be. Because of her circumstances, this means that she is tending to assert a modified form of traditional values in the face of a feminism to which she is fundamentally sympathetic. Zoe Fairbairns uses the colloquial, speaking voice because it provides her with the only kind of language that she can use for this purpose. No other variety of language would do the job so economically and so vividly.

In jamming these three voices together, the book allows all kinds of interesting cracks to appear. Conventional literary criticism emphasizes the logic of the book, its consistency. What emerges from this alternative reading, which invites the reader to refer outside the book itself to the way in which language contributes to the construction of a social reality, is its inconsistency. It should be stressed that the tension created between the public and private worlds is not a weakness of the book, it is at the heart of what Zoe Fairbairns is trying to say. What she is trying to represent is a whole knot of conflicting values that cannot be satisfactorily contained even by the conventional resort to irony. She knows how comfortable that would be.

Those conflicting values can be rather clumsily articulated along the following lines. History is the story of male hegemony, which denies women the opportunity to experience their full individuality. Organizing against this conspiracy requires collective action, which, by demanding submission to the will of others, is itself a poisoned chalice. Furthermore, it is part of their nature, as sexually defined, that women (like Lynn) have to be able to question even the beliefs that they hold most dear. Passionate conviction, blinkered self-interest, the ego in full flight, whatever you call it, is a male preserve. And yet only such powerful feeling is likely to serve as the mainspring of action, of change. By contrasting those different languages Zoe Fairbairns can convey these dilemmas as felt experience, as paradoxes that threaten, all the time, to bring the whole book crashing round her ears.

An analysis of this kind has much in common with the approach taken by Peter Stockwell in commenting on his short story *Tom's Last Voyage* (see Appendix A). Central to both are notions about language variety, and the social and cultural significance of particular kinds of language use. It is possible to find important points of contact between this and some of the more recent approaches being developed under the general title of 'Communication'.

8 Communication I: 'A' level Communication Studies

'Communication' has been accorded a chapter to itself as a way of acknowledging how the exam system has institutionalized the range of alternatives at 'A' level. Effectively, it has divided the world up into those who keep a tight hold of English Literature, angrily defending its special status, and those who, willing to venture beyond literature, are faced with a difficult choice between 'English Language' and 'Communications'. Realistically, there are not many other options, though some colleges are large enough to duck the problem by offering all three.

While there are perfectly understandable reasons why the post-GCSE English curriculum has come to be represented by a choice between these three subjects, the effect has not always been healthy. Between them, they have dictated the terms on which the curriculum debate should be conducted, and nowhere is this more true than in the general curriculum area variously designated as communication, media education or cultural studies. In the absence of any competitor the 'Communication Studies' 'A' syllabus has remained, in an important and damaging sense, uncontroversial. For this reason, it is important that the syllabus should not be thought beyond reproach, even though its pre-eminence has been, in some ways, well deserved.

'A' level Communication Studies

While the meaning of 'Communication Studies' at 'A' level has been exclusively that provided by the authors of the AEB syllabus, there have been changes in the 10 years since the subject was first introduced. The most significant of these took place in 1984 (for first examination in 1986) when the theoretical content of the syllabus was radically revised. It is possible to see the changes that were made as a direct response to some of the criticisms that had been levelled at the syllabus, and, therefore, as a convenient introduction to the ideological debate.

The original syllabus was the creation of lecturers in FE Colleges, not teachers in schools. And their influence is easily detected. It was the first 'A' level even remotely connected with English to allow a substantial element of practical work, or to require study of its own theoretical position. More importantly, it laid great stress on the relationship between theory and practice, defining the subject largely in terms of its applications.

In the early days, those who found it particularly attractive were often refugees from literature, who quickly developed a missionary zeal on behalf of the new subject. While there had been no formal intention to challenge the status quo, partisan feelings developed and some teachers and lecturers came to see 'Communication Studies' as a potential replacement for 'English Literature', and even, in a broader sense, communication as a replacement for English. They were impatient with what they considered the self-indulgence of much literary study, which, they felt, was inadequately theorized and increasingly irrelevant. Moreover, so the argument went, the broad appeal to literature as the embodiment of value, and its study as a humanizing influence, was no longer credible.

What 'Communication Studies' offered was a chance to replace the worthy intentions of English teachers with a model for curriculum design that was altogether more steely-eyed. In place of vague talk about 'maturity' and 'growth', there would be a quite close specification of the 'abilities' that students would have acquired by the end of the course. Take, for example, that part of the 'A' level syllabus concerned with the 'development of the students' abilities through practical work in the spoken, written and printed word and visual material'. Despite all the talk among English teachers about real contexts for writing, practice, it was argued, had not significantly changed. If, as was sometimes claimed, the culprit was an exam system that had failed to respond to changing perceptions about language, then the solution was obvious. Built into the requirements for 'Communication Studies', so that there could be no evasion, was the requirement that candidates should be able to 'appreciate the needs of a particular readership or audience' and 'write for specified levels of readership'. Only in this way, it was claimed, was it possible to provide the kind of rigour lacking in 'English'.

It is hardly surprising that the syllabus met with some criticism, or that this criticism originated from those English teachers whose practices were, implicitly at least, being questioned. Significantly, 'Communication Studies' responded not by isolating itself within a neat curriculum ghetto of its own, but by attempting to answer its critics. In this sense, the 1984 re-write was a confirmation that the advocates of communication really did see it as an eventual replacement for English, and if some modifications were required to convince others, then so be it. The general nature of the changes that were made is outlined in Fig. 7.

The theory appears in Paper 1, and it was here that most of the changes occurred. As a way of charting the boundaries of the subject, the original syllabus had established four discrete areas for study: 'Development of Communications', 'Theories of Communication', 'Mass Communications' and 'Means of Communication'. Unfortunately, there was no clear indication of how each of these might be related to each other. History was separated from Theory, and the

'A' level Communication Studies		
1st syllabus		2nd syllabus
Paper 1 – 40% 4 questions, 1 from each section: 1 Development of Communications 2 Theories of Communication 3 Mass Communication 4 Means of Communication		**Paper 1 – 40%** 4 questions, 1 from section A (general), 3 from section B (specific). A common content area: 1 Categories of Communication 2 Forms of Communication 3 Uses of Communication 4 Theory in Communication studies
Paper 2 – 30% Case study to apply theoretical study to given cases. Written and visual material seen by candidates 2 days before exam; Q's unseen		**Paper 2 – 30%** Case study to apply theoretical study to given cases. Written and visual materials seen by candidates 2 days before exam, Q's unseen
Project – 30% From choice of factual report, instruction manual, guide, TV programme, film, radio programme		**Project – 30%** Suggested: leaflet, booklet, magazine, tape-slide sequence, radio, TV programme, film, report, manual, guide
Oral examination 10% 20 – 30 min to discuss project		**Oral examination 10%** 10 min presentation to peers, followed by questions

Figure 7

study of mass media from other means of communication. The effect was to draw attention to a lack of any coherence in the subject.

By contrast, the re-written syllabus goes to great pains to create an integrated theory. The 'Further Notes for Guidance' puts it this way:

They [the candidates] will deal with individual topic areas. They should also be able to deal with these topics as they relate to one another. An example of such inter-relationship would emerge in a situation where two people are engaged in argument. The *forms* of communication involved would be verbal and non-verbal; the general *category* of communication would be that of the interpersonal; the *use* of communication would include exchange of information, and persuasion; study of *theory* of social interaction would illuminate what was happening. Thus the situation could be described and interpreted through study in all the content areas of the syllabus.

For an illustration of what this meant in practice, it is worth taking a look at the contrasting treatment of 'Mass Communications' in the two syllabuses. The separation, in the first version, of 'Mass Communication' from other media turned it into a special case. The parallel with English syllabuses in which literature is treated as a privileged form of writing is unmistakable. As a consequence, it was possible, at least in theory, to study the mass media as a set of ahistorical phenomena quite unaffected by the economic, social and cultural circumstances of the society in which they exist.

This view is borne out by the wording of the relevant part of the syllabus, which rejoiced in the promising, but ultimately hollow title of *Interaction between Media and Society Today*:

A study of the extent to which the media (a) generate, (b) influence, (c) interpret social change in the home, at work, in commerce and industry, in politics, education, and the arts.

The interaction was all one-way. If this seems to be overstating the case, take a look at the questions set on 'Mass Communication' in the 1985 examination paper:[1]

Section 3: Mass Communication

7 In an age of mass communication it is difficult for individuals to make public statements which have a broad influence.

How far would you agree with this statement?

Give examples from a range of mass media to support your argument.

(25 marks)

8 (a) How should the media of mass communications take account of the multi-cultural nature of British society?

(15 marks)

and

(b) To what extent have the media successfully discharged this obligation?

(10 marks)

9 Film is probably the most powerful propaganda medium yet devised. As a consequence, its potential for aiding or injuring civilisation is enormous.

(Agee, Ault and Emery, *Introduction to Mass Communications*, Harper and Ross, 7th Edn., 1982).

How far would you agree with the view of film when compared with either

(a) Television

or

(b) The Press

(25 marks)

Without exception, all the questions look at how the media exert influence without also considering how they reflect it. Question 8 is one of the worst culprits. By assuming that what pushes an issue on to the agenda is moral 'obligation', the wording of the question specifically excludes any discussion about the purchasing power of black communities, about access and ownership, or about organization and control. This is by no means an isolated example. Questions (7) and (9) have their origins in thinking of a similar kind. By encouraging candidates to think about the audience for 'public statements' made on television, (7) deflects attention from the rather more interesting issue of who appears on television and why. Question (9) is essentially the same. It focuses on the formal properties of different media and can, quite reasonably, be answered without reference to anything other than the technology of production. It would have been a more difficult, but a more interesting, question if it had required a comparison between, say, Channel 4 and the BBC.

The overriding preoccupation of questions like these is with *form*. An important consequence is that they assume a straightforward, common-sense relationship between the user and the medium. As if films, say, or newspapers, were tools in the sense that trowels or spades are, lying around waiting to be picked up and 'used' by people who wish to convey a 'message'. There is no obvious recognition of the way in which the media are themselves socially composed or, therefore, the extent to which they are responsible for determining the nature of the message.

By 1984, however, the relevant section of the syllabus read quite differently:

Categories of Communication	*Guidance Notes*
Mass Communication: including study of the mass media and of the institutions, characteristics, and effects of kinds of mass communication.	Includes such mass media as radio, television and the press and such concepts as access, control, audience, mediation and stereotyping.

The references to 'access' and 'control' would have been unthinkable 10 years earlier, and the introduction of 'stereotyping' as a key issue invites a much more sophisticated analysis of how meanings are made. The models of mass communication with which the examiners are prepared to work have become infinitely more complex, as this question from the 1986 paper exemplifies:[2]

2. The figure below is a diagram of a model of the process of mass communication.

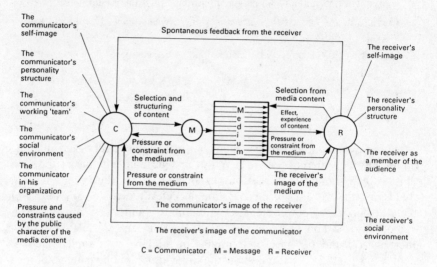

C = Communicator   M = Message   R = Receiver

What influence do the elements identified in this model have on the content of the mass media in contemporary Britain?

(25 marks)

Differences might exist about the relative importance of different influences within this model, and there might be some objections to the way in which the wording of the question does not allow it to be questioned, but there can be no mistaking the extent of the change.

It was not just the study of the mass media that took on a different appearance; other topics on the syllabus underwent an equally dramatic transformation. Two further examples might help to provide a more complete picture of the changing ideology of Communication Studies. The first of these is an addition. In a section devoted to 'Further Notes for Guidance', the introduction to the rewritten syllabus includes the following important phrase:

> The course as a whole will take account of the fact that we have learned to be receivers and users of communication, that it is what we have learned *and how we have learned it*, that is of significance.

The second is a reorganization. In the original syllabus 'the clarification of ideas through internal dialogue' is relegated to one item in a sub-section, 'The organisation and dissemination of information [sic]', of a sub-section, 'Processes'. In the new syllabus, 'Intrapersonal Communication' is allocated a sub-section of its own, having become a discrete category of communication. The accompanying description refers to the study of 'concepts such as . . . the generation of meanings' and elsewhere the syllabus concedes that the term 'information' may need defining so that its specialist use does not carry the instrumental overtones which would more normally be associated with it.

What had been recognized was that communication is an interactive process, and that individuals do not exist independently of the environment within which they are communicating. This made it possible to acknowledge that communicative behaviour is not just a question of shopping around for a set of appropriate techniques. It is determined by what people have learned, by what they are, and by what they want to say. In a theoretical sense, this new version of 'Communication Studies' was more cognitive, less behaviouristic. And by being more complex, it also became more flexible, opening up the possibility of a more empirical approach to the subject.

The claim that 'A' level Communication Studies was being smartened up for more general consumption probably has some truth in it. Certainly, mark 2 is less likely to scare off teachers with a background in literature, and this is an important point; although English teachers do not have exclusive rights on the syllabus, it tends, institutionally, to fall within their sphere of responsibility. The subject has come in from the cold, shedding some of its more aggressively utilitarian features, and recognizing a place for traditional concerns with personal development and 'growth'.

Some of the criticism levelled at the subject, however, was of the kind that can not be deflected by revising an examination syllabus. It originated from those English teachers who remained broadly committed to the tradition of Leavisite literary criticism. They had two related objections: one was that the subject lacked moral seriousness, the other, that it did not encourage discrimination. It is with horror that these critics report how students are actively dissuaded from making judgements about 'media texts'. Substitute 'Communication' for 'English' and serious writing, they claim, will be processed as if it could not be distinguished from advertising copy, the pursuit of Truth wantonly sacrificed to the categorization of ephemera.

This view was argued with some passion by Roger Knight, lecturer in Education at Leicester University, in the pages of *English in Education* (1982). He used the recent publication of Len Masterman's influential book *Teaching about Television* (1980) as an opportunity to open a wider debate.

In his reflections about the history of media education, Masterman makes much of the way in which, until recently, television has been largely ignored by the education system, pointing out that English teachers were often the most passionate critics of the medium. For many, television was the enemy, blunting the sensibility by promoting a debased culture. Far from being an object of study, it was a cause for concern, part of what provoked a missionary zeal to rescue the goggling classes from themselves. Where media education entered the classroom, it was by the back door, following the grudging concession that, occasionally, television could aspire to the condition of art, and that, when this happened, it might repay closer study. Deciding what was art, however, remained firmly the province of the literary critic, whose job it was to *discriminate*.

About such discrimination Masterman is scathing:[3]

> The very notion of discrimination is founded upon a distrust of what many pupils
> actually like, while the response implicit in 'appreciation' is essentially one of passive
> humility before an awesome tradition. Both words suggest acts of accommodation to
> an established culture rather than the honing of individual or group awareness.

It was this, and the accompanying assertion that the 'established culture' is
socially and historically specific, that fired Knight into the following polemic:

> I am not the first to remark that those who first gave the term currency were, in their
> practice, at pains to demonstrate that discrimination could transcend questions of
> social class. And this, of course, must follow if we are able to regard works of art as
> themselves transcending whatever class affiliations we may discern in them or other
> authors. Let Masterman read F. R. Leavis on 'Thought and Emotional Quality' or
> 'Reality and Sincerity' and see whether he can unblushingly attribute them simply to
> a 'bourgeois hegemony'. For *there* is discrimination at its exemplary and directive
> best, the critic urging us through the familiar critical procedure to see this rather than
> that poem as spiritually finer, more worthy of our attention.

The language of that final sentence is entirely characteristic, not just of Knight,
but of the whole system of belief that he so unswervingly represents. In a second
piece, replying to Len Masterman's defence of his position, Roger Knight
illustrates his point by a lengthy account of how, with a group of sixth formers, he
worked on D. J. Enright's poem *A Polished Performance*. He concludes by listing
the questions that 'encourage discrimination':

> How *truthful* are the ironies of Enright's poem? When we consult our own
> experience, our own considered view of the world and our uses of language, how
> *troubling or diverting* – do we find his play with words and the criticism they express?
> [my italics].[4]

This is a very revealing passage, partly because the language draws attention so
precisely to the shortcomings of the critical system that is being defended.
Literature is construed as a kind of instrument for puncturing the reader's
complacency, charming either because it is painless or because, like any other
diversion, it is easily ignored. Literary judgements, it is argued, depend upon
whether or not the work being studied is considered 'truthful'. And in order to
determine this, we are advised to 'consult our own experience'. What Roger
Knight fails to acknowledge is the way in which the reader's experience is socially
constituted. Even 18-year-olds are not the kind of innocent readers that are
imagined here, entirely credulous about every work of literature they encounter,
nor should they be.

What Knight is actually doing is claiming for one highly specific set of values,
the status of 'truth', and reinforcing this by insisting that no other way of
discriminating is possible. The reason why media education finds it hard to
answer this kind of criticism is that the subject is being asked to defend itself for
not being what it is not, namely, English Literature. It is for this reason that Roger

Knight fails to realize how badly he has damaged his own argument when he quotes the following passage from 'Teaching about Television' (1984): '. . . judgement can be suspended and mass media material simply examined – seen more clearly – so that a *wider and more complex range of meaning and values* can become apparent . . .'. While he is trying to direct our attention towards the damaging admission that 'judgement can be suspended', the eye is irresistibly drawn to that other phrase about how 'a wider and more complex range of meaning and values can become apparent'.

In a more recent publication, *Teaching Popular Television*, Mike Clarke (1987) describes the controversy as 'a curious form of shadow boxing', pointing out that everybody is quite properly committed to 'some form of evaluation'. The important questions that need asking are about 'what the basis of this should be':

> Looked at in a perhaps more commonsense way, the question becomes: what kind of arguments can be advanced for the judgments we all routinely make? Are such judgments inescapably partial, dependent on whim or political allegiance, for example?

In practice, it is neither possible nor desirable, when discussing texts, to purge our language of everything that might smack of 'the judgements we all routinely make'. And that is not, to be fair, what is being proposed. Consider these questions, for example, which were included in 'A' level Communication Studies papers:[5]

> 'Advertisements are selling us something more than consumer goods. In providing us with a structure in which we and those goods are interchangeable, they are selling us ourselves.' Judith Williamson, 'Decoding Advertisements' 1978, London, M. Boyars.

> In the light of this opinion, to what extent do you think that advertisers in magazines and on television use and manipulate the self-image of potential customers?

While an answer to this question would almost certainly focus largely on *technique*, the choice of the word 'manipulate', with its suggestion that such techniques are unscrupulous, invites some discussion about the ethics of advertising.

Any accusation that this question is uncharacteristic ought to be dispelled by question 5 in the same paper:[6]

> 'People are that which their relationships allow them to become.' (Professor David Jenkins, Bishop of Durham)

> To what extent would you regard the quality of personal relationships and the quality of interpersonal communication as being interdependent?

Roger Knight may not relish the kind of language in which such a discussion would be conducted, but he would find it hard to deny that students are being asked to engage with ethical, and other, questions about the 'quality' of their experience.

The point that both Len Masterman and Mike Clarke are making about judgement is that it must be open; it must concede its assumptions and make available to others the routes by which it has been reached. It is fair to say that this position now attracts a measure of agreement across the whole range of courses in Film Studies, Media Education, and Communications. It is what informs the kind of question at 'A' level that is exemplified by the following:[7]

> To what extent do semiotics provide a useful perspective for the study of
>
> (a) propaganda
>
> AND
>
> (b) popular culture?

It is one of the things that are lacking in the study of literature at 'A' level, a shortcoming which helps to account for the kind of mess that was described in Chapters 2 and 3. In this sense, though not in others, 'Communication Studies' has got it right.

9 Communication II: beyond Communication Studies

Despite all its virtues, despite the real enthusiasm that the subject can generate, despite the imaginative 'case study' papers, despite the opportunities provided by the project to engage with real problems worth solving, 'A' level Communication Studies is still seriously flawed. Even though the re-written syllabus seems to have got all the angles covered and the critics have been answered, doubts remain.

Put bluntly, the subject remains vulnerable to the charge that it is reductive. The nature of the problem can best be illustrated by asking how well the theoretical framework of the syllabus is able to handle complex utterances. Or, an alternative version of the same question, with what degree of complexity it can describe apparently simple ones. In order to illustrate how their new unified theory might work in practice, the authors of the revised syllabus neatly parcelled up 'a situation where two people are engaged in argument' by reference to *forms, categories, uses and theories* of communication. It was done with sufficient flair to distract attention from the awkward question of whether the theory was more widely applicable. Could the same be done, say, for a situation where one person is engaged in writing a poem?

Take *To His Coy Mistress* by Andrew Marvell. The *form* of the communication is, uncontroversially, 'written and printed'. At least, it is for the twentieth-century reader. For its original audiences, it was never printed and was circulated in a much less formal sense than we might recognize today. It is equally difficult to find a *category* that adequately represents the poem as a type of communication. Is, for example:

> Had we but world enough and time
> This coyness, lady, were no crime.

'interpersonal' or 'mass' communication? Or did the 'lady' exist at all? Is it 'Intrapersonal' communication on a grand scale? Either way, the important questions about the poem, and, more generally, about Marvell as a writer, do not get asked. More illuminating might be some sense of the circumstances within which Marvell wrote, and the audience that he was addressing. A serious analysis would need to find some way of teasing out, for example, the implications of the fact that his contemporary reputation was as a public figure, and author of satirical pamphlets and that the poetry for which he is now best known was not published until after his death. It implies a set of assumptions about literary production that are quite alien to twentieth-century culture.

Questions about the *use* of such a piece of communication seem equally inappropriate. The 'A' level syllabus offers a number of 'uses' that include reference to 'the arts' – 'entertainment', or, more improbably, 'social functioning' – but they all inevitably assume that a poem actually has a 'use'. Even a label like 'creative expression in the arts' (a sub-set of 'social functioning'), linked as it is to notions like 'personal development' or 'self-expression', seems to imply that writing poetry fulfils some kind of temperamental need. As a version of what he was doing, Marvell would have found it all quite bemusing.

A fuller sense than communications theory can provide of the range and complexity of the issues that need taking into account when dealing with a piece of literature like a poem is provided by Raymond Williams (1981) in *Culture*. In trying to map out a sociology of culture, what Williams makes plain is the subtlety of the relationship between cultural activity and the society in which it takes place. His success in doing this can be attributed in part to his skill in making fine distinctions based upon real cases; it also derives from his ideological commitment to particular kinds of historical analysis.

It is these two features of Williams' work that are missing in the 'Communication Studies' 'A' level, and which makes the theoretical framework of the syllabus ultimately disappointing. The two points deserve separate treatment.

First, then, the question of how the theory is derived. Structurally, the 'A' level syllabus isolates the theory (Paper 1, general questions) from its applications (Paper 2, case studies). This separation allows it to be described, and even, potentially, acquired, as a body of prepackaged knowledge, rather than as a series of working hypotheses. It increases the risk that it will be used more like a template than a blueprint. Actual instances of communication make an appearance not as the raw material of investigations, but as appropriate illustrations for the general theory.

Before the authors of the syllabus cry 'foul', it should be acknowledged that candidates are sometimes invited to analyse particular examples of communication in the case study paper. Case studies, however, do not provide an ideal vehicle for work of this kind. Because the whole point of a case study is to create a context for the student to operate in role, the kind of analytical comments that it is appropriate to make are circumscribed by that role. This point might be more easily explained with an illustration.

The 1986 paper included a case study called 'Microwriter' in which candidates were asked, among other things, to 'write a 500 word evaluation' of material issued by the company which manufactures Microwriter. This material is described in an accompanying letter as an 'informational' leaflet; part of which is reproduced as Fig. 8. One of the most interesting things about this leaflet as a piece of communication is the way in which it blurs the distinction between advertising and information. The question and answer format, limited range of colour, sober typeface, and absence of obvious marketing ploys are all designed to indicate a serious intention to inform rather than persuade. The message that is conveyed by the language, however, is quite at odds with this. At times it apes advertising copy in a way that seems almost transparent: 'new and unique . . . the world's first . . . a remarkably powerful machine . . .'. Elsewhere, it adopts a colloquial style that is intended to be reassuring and direct, but which is also immediately recognizable as the authentic voice of the salesman: 'don't be misled . . . Quite simply . . . Take a look . . . it's easier than falling off a log . . .'.

For the candidates, there is no real problem. The instructions which they have been given stress that the report must 'include creative constructive suggestions', which are going to appeal to Microwriter who are 'a bit touchy' about one or two features of the product. Moreover, it is made quite clear to the candidates that their own commercial success depends upon whether they can persuade Microwriter to offer them (trainee copywriters at PCPR) the marketing contract. Success probably depends upon the production of a report that further obscures the distinction between information and advertising copy. It is just that aspect of the material, however, that a more dispassionate analysis of how it functions as a piece of communication would find of special interest.

Because the syllabus has no natural home for this kind of 'Communications in Use', the theory that it promotes remains too mechanistic, too inflexible. This objection to the syllabus leads on naturally to the second point that was suggested by the comparison with the work undertaken by Raymond Williams in *Culture*, that the theory is historically naive.

Where the syllabus directly addresses the history of communications, it provides for:

> Description and interpretation of the development of mass communications from the late nineteenth century and of the significance of this for contemporary society, and for the future.

The exam papers provide questions that can reasonably be taken as an interpretation of this paragraph:

> How far does your study of the development of communications lead you to believe that adequate communication between groups is necessary for social progress?[1]

> How is the developing technology of computer graphics opening up fresh horizons for scientists, designers and creative artists alike?[2]

What both questions are preoccupied with is the technology of communications. This approach allows the 'history' in the syllabus to be about communications *systems*, not about the way in which communications are historically constituted. The tidy packages – 'group interaction', 'computer graphics' – that it creates can all be studied for the way in which they have 'developed', with sublime

MICROWRITER
WRITE INTO TYPE

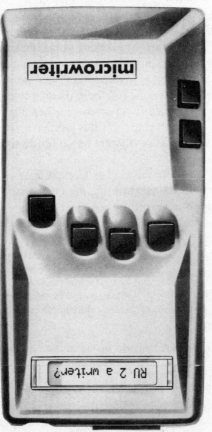

"WHAT IS A MICROWRITER?"

'Newsweek' said it all when they wrote – "The Microwriter is ... a replacement for every known method of putting thoughts onto paper."

Using the new and unique five-finger keyboard, the Microwriter supersedes handwriting, dictation and the typewriter as a means of originating text – the world's first fully portable word processor. The Microwriter can be used as an input device to your existing micro-computer or word processor.

"WHAT'S IT FOR?"

Think of the amount of writing you do in a working day – letters, memos, reports, speeches, notes, etc. A Micro-writer will cope with the lot.

Normally you'd originate text by hand, or perhaps by dictation. Then you wait for it to be rewritten on a typewriter, possibly sending it back for correction.

By producing that copy on a Microwriter you'll eliminate the duplication of effort and the frustration of redrafting.

And because it's portable it's just as invaluable at home or out in the field.

"WHAT DOES IT DO?"

Although it's no bigger than an average paperback book, don't be misled. The Microwriter is a remarkably powerful machine.

Quite simply, its six keys have the capabilities of the entire typewriter keyboard.

It will produce both upper and lower case alphabets, numerals, the full range of punctuation, as well as an additional range of technical symbols.

As you produce your copy, it's stored on a 1600 word memory – that's about five pages of A4. Once there it can be recalled on the moving display of any time, allowing you to make corrections or insertions.

Plug the Microwriter into a printer or electronic typewriter and your copy is immediately transformed into neatly typed text.

You're not limited in your choice of formats. The Microwriter easily copes with standard and variable formats on any size or type of paper, including automatic carriage returns, indented paragraphs, headings, underlining and complex tabulations.

All this the Microwriter will do with just the help of a printer. A television monitor can be used to increase the display. Take a look at

"HOW FRIENDLY IS THE MICROWRITER TO OTHER EQUIPMENT?"

The Microwriter's compatibility with other equipment gives you a powerful means of access to systems in use everywhere.

It's compatible with most standard RS232C equipment, capable of both transmitting and receiving data. It can also be used as an alternative keyboard on most KSR and RO printers using this standard.

the top right hand section of this sheet and you'll see how well it interfaces with other equipment, enhancing its own capabilities.

"BUT ISN'T IT HARD TO LEARN?"

No, quite the contr .y. Thousands of users have proved that Microwriting can be learned in an hour or less, and that you can be producing work within a day. In a few days of practice you can reach handwriting speed. With regular use you'll be Microwriting more than twice as fast as you can handle a pen.

Compared to the months it takes to train a typist, it's easier than falling off a log.

Take a look at the "New User's Guide" that comes with this package and prove that you can use a Microwriter.

"WHAT ABOUT SALES AND SERVICE?"

Rest assured that from the moment you first buy your Microwriter, you will receive a professional and efficient service directly from Microwriter Ltd.

You may well be thinking of buying other equipment to use with your Microwriter. Microwriter Ltd can supply or advise on the wide range of hardware and software that's available.

Figure 8

indifference to social circumstances. There is an interesting parallel to be drawn with the way in which conventional literary criticism places a stress on 'tradition' as the way to arrive at an understanding of literary form. What 'tradition' offers is a self-contained world in which the only influences at work on writers are other writers. 'Communications' as it is defined here offers much the same opportunities to fall into much the same traps.

One final point needs to be made about the syllabus which might help to clinch the argument. By and large, this survey has concentrated on the theory in Paper 1. For anybody unfamiliar with the syllabus, this will have proved to be something of a distorting lens. The explicit theory, after all, is only 40 per cent of the marks, and much that is most exciting about the syllabus is contained in the Case Study Paper, and the Project. It is here, though, in the Project, that there is a further indication of how the syllabus, even in its re-written form, still has some significant shortcomings.

The first syllabus was quite specific about the kind of 'Project' that it was legitimate to produce. There were six categories, four of which were very tightly defined indeed. If you were planning to produce something in a conventional printed (written) form, then it had to be a 'factual report', an 'instruction manual' or a 'guide'. Even within the limited definition of communication that the syllabus had provided, this was a narrow range of possibilities. The other two categories appeared to offer more scope – 'A Television Programme or a Film' and 'A Sound Radio Programme' – and, in practice, they did allow greater diversity. One suspects, however, that they were originally included simply in order to vary the choice of media in which candidates could work, and not for any other reason.

The new syllabus dispenses with this kind of central control by the Exam Board – 'the subject, form or structure of the work is not prescribed'. The field, it seems, is wide open. There is inevitably a question, however, about whether the syllabus would accept or could cope with, say, any of the following: a sonnet cycle, an extract from a novel, a subjective documentary, autobiography, a rock video, a computer game, and so on. Nothing in the rest of the course suggests how any of these could be assessed. To put it differently, if they were assessed in a way that conformed to the theory in Paper 1, something important about them would be ignored.

At the beginning of this chapter, a distinction was drawn between communication and the particular version of it that is enshrined in the AEB syllabus. Before moving on, it is worth returning to that distinction if only because the subsequent direction of the argument has obscured the existence of other possible contenders for a place in the post-16 curriculum. A looser definition of communication might have opened the way for discussion of 'A' level Theatre Studies, and 'A' level Film Studies. A lengthy account of either of them would be too specialized to remain of general interest here. However, their very existence does help to provide a further illustration of what is happening in the gap created by dissatisfaction with 'A' English Literature. It also highlights how different from 'English literature' are some of the alternatives on offer, even where they remain strictly experimental. This last point is made in Peter Womack's (1987) paper *Changing A-Levels*. He writes about:

> the challenge which is inevitably confronting sixth form English because of its new bedfellows. Text, in both theatre and communication models, is insistently a functional and context-specific performance. Drama students are not supposed to abstract playscripts from the multiple constraints of presentation – this is played to whom? for what agreed purpose? according to what conventions? in what kind of space? And for Communication Studies it's axiomatic that an utterance of any kind is produced within a set of communicative rules, whether these are conceived be-haviouristically or semiotically. Clearly students who are learning to think such mediations are going to find it increasingly difficult to believe in the simple, immediate textual presence which is the traditional object of literary criticism.

For those who have had their perceptions shaped by some of the new syllabuses described in this chapter, there is no going back. The special status of 'English literature' has gone forever.

For English teachers, there are a number of ways in which they can respond. Two specific examples are sufficient to indicate some of the range of possibilities. The first is taken from *English Teaching since 1965: How much Growth?* by David Allen (1980). Allen's book can reasonably be described as an attempt to reconcile a broadly Leavisite position on English teaching with the realities of post-1960s comprehensive education. In the last few chapters, a note of resignation creeps in, as if David Allen knows that, whatever he may say, English teaching is developing in ways that make him profoundly uneasy. The culprit, of course, is communication. He sees arising from the movement to treat literature as a form of language, a similar pressure to treat language as simply a form of communi-cation. 'Presumably', he writes, 'in such a growth, there may be a new danger that language is treated as merely one among equals. This is a debate to be heard in the next few years in the field of English 16–19.' His remedy is a simple one, a return to what is 'distinctive' about English:

> I want to insist that not all our language is worth our attention – or on the other hand some kinds of human utterance are worth more than others, and of these, the one I see as characterising English is that of *art-speech*, in which I include the novel, poem, play, autobiography (whether created or received, silent or aloud, public or private). Literature is a vital part of it, but not all of it, since art-speech includes creation as well as reception.

That was published in 1980, but already it seems like whistling in the wind. As a policy on media education and communication studies, it provides nothing more than the hope that if you close your eyes, it will all go away.

A more positive response is provided by those advocates of communications who still wish to remain within the general orbit of 'English teaching'. A succinct account of their position is included in the *English in Education* 'Teaching about television debate'. Four lecturers in higher education at the Polytechnic of Wales made a helpful contribution which, like David Allen's book, looked at the position of communications in relation to more traditional understandings about English. It will come as no surprise that they reach very different conclusions:[3]

> Taking the 'theory' first, it can be argued that English and Media Studies are, far from incompatible opposites, actually concerned with the same object of study, namely the social production of meaning. But whereas English (literary) studies has been colonised, as it were, by the discourse of discrimination, and therefore addresses itself primarily to questions of individual creativity and response, Media Studies has been colonised by political and sociological discourses, and therefore relates meaning to their social purposes and uses and to their/the mode of production.

This description is a broadly accurate one, and certainly helps to explain why some of the discussion about media education leaves many English teachers untouched. Both the Wales Poly Communications team and Len Masterman have their solutions. The passage quoted above continues as follows:[4]

> A useful trade between these two colonies of Meaning should begin at once. Textual analysis can be exported from literary studies to analyse non-literary texts (this trade has been going on for years beyond the horizons of school-English). Conversely, English needs to import Media/Cultural Studies' attention to the relations between the production of meaning and the reproduction of social stratification and sub-ordination.

Masterman makes the same point in a rather more challenging way:[5]

> The general failure of English teachers over the past decade to gain any critical purchase upon television has delivered much media education into the hands of the sociologists, a development which, in spite of the proliferation of a good deal of mystificatory jargon, has been a progressive one. If English teachers are to re-enter the debate they must learn from past mistakes. They can bring to media education both pedagogic sophistication and a much needed rigour in the analysis of media texts.

It is difficult to know exactly what Len Masterman had in mind when he delivered that rebuke. What he got was a wholesale redefinition of the subject. In seeking to 're-enter the debate', English teachers also changed the terms on which it was being conducted. Subjected to the scrutiny of literary criticism, media education becomes cultural studies.

The Summer 1989 edition of *The English Magazine* appeared with an article, 'Challenging "A" level', in which Steve Bennison and Andrew Spicer described an 'A' level syllabus devised by the Avon NATE branch. They introduced their 'dream syllabus' in the following way:

> Our starting point was to see the whole area of cultural production and reception as a single unified field, and to gather together the most progressive elements in all the relevant existing syllabuses, whatever their particular label. The aim, however, was not to produce a compromise, but to incorporate these elements within a fundamentally rethought framework, based on a set of core concepts which we hoped would provide the syllabus with a distinctive, coherent philosophy.

The thread that links this with media education is quite clear. The reference to 'cultural production and reception' echoes the language of the lecturers in communication at the Polytechnic of Wales when they talk about 'the social production of meaning'. The exclusive concern with media texts, however, has been replaced by a broader interest in all forms of cultural production and a theory has been embraced that can account for both 'high art and popular culture' in a way that 'Communication Studies' never managed.

Two features of the syllabus that have resulted from this are particularly impressive. The first is that a way has been found, in the 'core concepts', of boiling down into something more manageable the great mass of ideas currently being generated within 'English Studies'. The second is the production of 'outline modules' which help to make possible a realization of the kind of work that is based upon 'abstract theory' while resisting any suggestion that it ought to be taught. Despite this achievement, however, the syllabus also illustrates just how difficult it is to translate Raymond Williams' ideas in *Culture* into a form that is not only accessible at 'A' level, but capable of attracting widespread support. The syllabus that appeared in *The English Magazine* has since been re-written. It appears here in a more recent form following discussions with the London Examinations Board. It should be noted that this is an abbreviated version of the complete syllabus.

Introduction

This syllabus encompasses the areas of study traditionally designated English Language and Literature, Media Studies, Theatre Studies and Communication, as well as the study of other areas of cultural practice. 'Cultural Studies' is therefore seen here as involving both 'high' art and popular culture. Within this syllabus, however, this is recognised as a single field of study, unified by a set of core concepts, thus leading to the development of a broad knowledge and understanding with a theoretically informed focus and coherence. The syllabus specifies a wide range of material and activities, and involves skills of investigation and analysis, production and presentation. In its scope, structure and methods of assessment, it provides a logical progression from GCSE and prepares candidates for recent developments in HE and current trends in employment. Its modular structure allows for flexible timetabling, with a notional 300 hours of lesson-time plus additional study leading to an A Level qualification, 150 hours to AS Level. Through the establishment of consortia, the syllabus ensures the close and continuing involvement of practising teachers, in the maintenance of high standards and in further development of the range of work undertaken.

Aims and Objectives

- This syllabus aims to enable candidates to develop a broad knowledge and understanding, through investigating and analysing cultural practices of all kinds.
- The aim of the syllabus is that this will be given a theoretically informed focus and coherence through the use of the following four inter-related core concepts which, together, explain the processes through which cultural practices operate and how they might be challenged or changed. It is intended that candidates will come to understand how, in each case, these processes are determined by

dominant and oppositional ideologies which are in turn determined by a wider social and political history.

a. *Form*: The meanings of cultural products are constructed through particular combinations of codes and conventions. An important aspect of this is the representation, including stereotyping, of people, places, events and ideas.

b. *Production*: Cultural products are produced and distributed within particular systems of ownership and organisation, utilising available materials and technology.

c. *Reproduction*: Cultural products are interpreted and adapted in particular educational, artistic and commercial practices.

d. *Reception*: Cultural products are understood differently by specific social groups in a particular place and time.

- This knowledge and understanding will inevitably work against bias and prejudice of any kind, including sexism and racism, by allowing a deeper appreciation of its nature and consequences.
- This syllabus aims primarily to develop skills of conceptualised investigation and analysis, but also of production and presentation.
- Candidates will be expected to investigate and analyse a range of cultural practices by applying the core concepts in:
  a. Close textual analysis
  b. Detailed consideration of wider issues, involving reading and research
- This will be demonstrated and assessed through:
  a. Conventional academic writing
  b. Work in a variety of other forms
  c. Oral presentation

Assessment Structure

A Level

Candidates will be assessed on a folder containing 6 units of coursework, one each from the Introductory Module, 4 Optional Modules and an Individual Module; on an oral presentation based on the Individual Module; and on the Final Module examination. These will be weighted as follows:

Introductory Module	10%	Approx. 30 hours of lesson-time
4 Optional Modules	4×10=40%	Approx. 4×30=120 hours of lesson-time
Individual Module	20%	Approx. 60 hours of lesson-time
Oral Presentation	10%	Approx. 30 hours of lesson-time
Final Module	20%	Approx. 60 hours of lesson-time
Total	100%	Approx. 300 hours of lesson-time

AS Level

Candidates will be assessed on a folder containing 3 units of coursework, one each from the Introductory Module and 2 Optional Modules; and on the Final Module examination. These will be weighted as follows:

Introductory Module	20%	Approx. 30 hours of lesson-time
2 Optional Modules	2×20=40%	Approx. 2×30=60 hours of lesson-time
Final Module	40%	Approx. 60 hours of lesson-time
Total	100%	Approx. 150 hours of lesson-time

Assessment Procedure

a. *Individual Module*: Coursework will be teacher-assessed, with internal standard-isation within centres and consortium moderation, subject to final approval by the Board Moderator.

b. *Optional Modules*: Coursework will be teacher-assessed, with internal standard-isation within centres and consortium moderation, subject to final approval by the Board Moderator.

c. *Individual Module*: Coursework and Oral Presentation will both be teacher-assessed, with internal standardisation within centres, subject to moderation by the Board Moderator visiting centres during the Spring Term of the 2nd year.

d. *Final Module*: Examination material and tasks will be set and assessed externally.

Forms of Coursework

- The primary objective of each unit of coursework should be to demonstrate a knowledge and understanding of the topic studied during the module, using the core concepts, but all coursework should also be designed for a particular audience to achieve a specific purpose.

- Candidates will submit coursework in both of the following 2 forms:

  a. *Conventional Academic Writing*: Essay, report, commentary, analysis.

  b. *Other Forms*: These will include poetry, narrative, playscript, autobiography, biography, creative extension of existing text, tape, tape-slide, video, radio programme, magazine, photo-essay, taped and transcribed interview, an-thology, advertising campaign material, exhibition, teaching pack, adaptation from one media into another.

Introductory Module

- This module requires candidates to apply the core concepts in a study of autobiography and the construction of subjectivity.

- Centres will be provided with sample teaching material, suggested activities and recommendations for further reading. This material will be regularly revised by the Board Moderator in the light of comments from centres.

- This module will thus provide a model for both teachers and candidates, initiating an analysis of some centrally important issues, which subsequent modules will then extend to other topics.

- Candidates will submit one unit of coursework of approx. 2000–2500 words. Either of the two forms of coursework will be acceptable, but must involve the application of at least one of the core concepts. This will be accompanied by an introduction of approx. 250 words, explaining its aims in terms of the core concepts, which will be taken into account in assessment.

Optional Modules

- The Optional Modules allow centres to construct a coherent course, using the core concepts to build on the approaches and issues initiated in the Introductory Module and, indirectly, to prepare candidates for the Individual and Final Modules. Centres are free to select as wide or specific a range of topics as they wish, appropriate to the needs of their particular candidates, responsive to special interests, and utilising available expertise and resources.

- The list of example modules . . . suggests some possible topics and indicates the use of the core concepts in some possible approaches. Centres are encouraged to construct their own modules, along similar lines and involving an equivalent amount of work, subject to discussion in consortia and final approval by the Board Moderator. It is envisaged that consortia will gradually develop a bank of material for Optional Modules which centres could draw on and contribute to.
- *A Level*: Four Optional Modules will be completed. For each module, candidates will submit one unit of coursework of approx. 2000–2500 words. Two units must be drawn from one of the forms of coursework and two from the other. Each must involve the application of at least one of the core concepts and all four core concepts must be used at least once. Each unit will be accompanied by an introduction of approx. 250 words, explaining its aims in terms of the core concepts, which will be taken into account in assessment.

  AS Level: Two Optional Modules will be completed. For each module, candidates will submit one unit of coursework of approx. 2000–2500 words. One unit must be drawn from one of the forms of coursework and one from the other. Each must involve the application of at least one of the core concepts and all four core concepts must be used at least once. Each unit will be accompanied by an introduction of approx. 250 words, explaining its aims in terms of the core concepts, which will be taken into account in assessment.

Individual Module

- This module offers candidates the opportunity to undertake an independent study of a topic of their own choice, using the core concepts.
- The list of example modules . . . may provide some suitable topics, but candidates are free to propose their own, subject to approval by the Board Moderator.
- Teachers should advise, assist and encourage this study and help candidates to obtain relevant material, but should not dictate the choice of or approach to the topic.
- Candidates will submit one unit of coursework of approx. 3000–3500 words. Either of the two forms of coursework will be acceptable, but must involve the application of all four core concepts. This will be accompanied by a logbook, explaining its aims in terms of the core concepts, recording work done and reflecting on learning achieved, which will be taken into account in assessment.
- During the Spring Term of their 2nd year, candidates will be required to give a 10 minute oral presentation, based on this work, to a group of their peers.

Final Module

- This module serves as a standard control component within the syllabus, while avoiding some of the constraints of a more conventional examination.
- During the Spring Term of their 2nd year, candidates will be provided with material for the study of a specified topic, of similar range and depth to an Optional Module.
- Centres will be provided with additional material and a suggested framework for this study, using the core concepts.
- Candidates will be assessed by means of a one-day six-hour examination. They will be expected to take in the material provided, together with additional material and preparatory work, but all work to be assessed will be completed under

examination conditions. Specific tasks will be issued on the day, and will involve both critical analysis and substantial creative re-working of the material provided, both requiring the application of the core concepts.

Example Modules

- Listed here is a representative selection of possible topics for Optional and Individual Modules, together with some indication as to how the core concepts might be used in possible methods and approaches. This list is intended to demonstrate the range, nature and amount of work envisaged. It should not be seen as exhaustive or exclusive.
- For the sake of comparison, this list is divided into categories familiar from existing A Level syllabuses, but it should be strongly emphasised that in this syllabus these areas are recognised as constituting a single field of study.

Literature

Study of a Genre: e.g. Romance, looking at Jane Eyre, Mills & Boon, teenage fiction, magazines, and perhaps also films, TV soaps, adverts etc., focusing on two such texts and applying the core concepts in considering such issues as narrative codes and conventions, the construction of the family, gender and sexuality, marketing and audience, differential and oppositional readings.

Further Examples: Some Representations of Madness in 19th Century Novels; The Construction of a Sense of Place in Recent Northern Irish Poetry; The Treatment of Class and Class-Conflict in Two Dickens Novels; Reworking of Generic Conventions in Recent Feminist Detective Novels; Representation of Childhood in a Selection of Local Community Publishing.

Media

Propaganda: looking at selected examples from a range of media, both verbal and visual, e.g. war films, political broadcasts, health campaigns etc., and using the core concepts to consider such issues as representations of race, nationality, justice and truth, effectiveness with specific audiences, conflicting definitions in relation to documentary and 'art'.

Further Examples: The Construction of Community in Two Current British Soap-Operas; A Film-Star as a Social Phenomenon; Newspaper, Magazine and TV Treatment of the Royal Family; Intertextuality in Recent Advertising; The Demonisation of Women in Film Noir.

Language

Study of a Dialect: looking at examples published or recorded or specially collected, and applying the core concepts in a consideration of such factors as roots and origins, syntactical, grammatical and phonetic features, variant forms and changing status in different social contexts.

Further Examples: Language for Learning in a Local Primary School; Some Uses of Dialect in Literature; Political Rhetoric; The Language of Religion; Language Acquisition & Development in Young Children.

Theatre

Study of a Play in its Historical Contexts: e.g. The Tempest, applying the core concepts in a consideration of such factors as its original staging and audiences, its use of blank verse, masque conventions and theatrical effects, its representation and reworking of

16th century colonialism, its reproduction as film and set-text, its role in the construction of Shakespeare as a national cultural institution.

Further Examples: The TV and Theatre Work of One Playwright Compared; Audience Reception of a Season of Plays at a Local Theatre; 19th Century Melodrama; Brechtian Theory in the Work of a Modern British Playwright.

Other Areas

Study of an Artistic Movement: e.g. Romanticism, concentrating on one writer or painter and selected critical writing, and examining through the core concepts such issues as ideologies of nature, childhood, industrialism, subjectivity, ideas of the artist as iconoclast and outsider, generic forms such as the lyric, gothic novels and landscape painting, the marketing of Grasmere.

Study of a Place: e.g. a local tourist resort, applying the core concepts in an analysis of such features as the ownership and organisation of facilities, social status of different areas of accommodation and entertainment, historical development, reproduction in advertising, guidebooks and travel-writing, views of councillors, shopkeepers, local people and tourists.

Study of a Period: e.g. The 1950s, looking at a selection of films, novels, plays, music, TV, advertising, journalism and cultural criticism from the period, and using the core concepts to consider such factors as representations of social change and social problems, the development of mass-marketing; the attempted assimilation of Caribbean immigrants; emergent forms of writing, theatre and film; ideologies of leisure, classlessness, affluence and consumerism; dominant notions of masculinity and the marginalisation of women; recent reproductions of the period in films, fashion, advertising, politics.

Study of a Popular Fictional Hero: e.g. James Bond or Sherlock Holmes, looking at his original literary construction and subsequent reproduction in films, TV series, newspaper serialisations, and commercial artefacts, and using the core concepts to consider such issues as changing ideologies of Englishness, crime and justice, masculinity and bachelor-dom; narrative formulae, setting and characterisation; mass-marketing and the creation of a popular myth.

Study of an Event: e.g. The 1984–5 Miners Strike, looking at diaries, songs, letters, poetry by miners and their wives, photographs, posters and ephemera, newspaper, magazine, TV, radio and film reporting, political speeches, retrospective autobiography and analysis, and using the core concepts to explore such issues as traditional ideas of community; the 'economics' of the industry; the mobilisation of popular support; the role of women; the construction of Scargill and McGregor as mythical combatants; the management of 'law and order'; reconstructions of the event as historical watershed.

10 Conclusion

Caution advises against this concluding chapter. There was a time when it was possible to speculate about future trends in education without running too much risk of being proved wrong. The rate of change is now so great, and the direction so unpredictable, that any attempt to look ahead is fraught with difficulty. When the government cannot make up its mind whether it wants to promote traditional 'standards', or to establish a curriculum for a new technological future, all that can be said with any certainty is that policy will change from day to day.

The rejection of the recommendations made by the Higginson Committee for a reform of 'A' level has done nothing to convince anybody that the government now knows what it wants. Far from stifling speculation, it has fanned the flames, and there is a substantial body of opinion that sees in the rejection of Higginson a green light for the examination boards to move ahead with their own plans. What this suggests is that the pressures for change have become so great that the government cannot keep things as they are merely by slapping a veto on plans for structural reform. If it really wants nothing to happen, then it will have to take active steps to ensure that it does not.

The pressure for change

Perhaps the most surprising feature of the Higginson Report was not that it received such a summary dismissal, but that it recommended such sweeping reform. Clear signals had been given long before the report was finally published that the government wanted 'A' level to stay roughly as it is. The committee, however, had become sufficiently alarmed about what John Banham of the CBI called 'a demographic time-bomb for skilled manpower' to exceed its brief. This is how the *Guardian* put it:[1]

> In fact Higginson reported at the very moment when employers, higher education and even the Government were becoming acutely aware of the difficulties facing them as the number of school leavers begins its 35% decline. One in four employers

are now facing skill shortages, according to the CBI, which was quick to condemn the precipitate rejection of Higginson . . .

The problem, in fact, is about to become more acute. The number of graduates is set to fall by the mid 90s – in spite of Kenneth Baker's commitment to raising the age participation rate from 14–18 percent. And probably in spite of higher education's best efforts to recruit more students from non-traditional groups such as ethnic minorities, women and the older age groups. At the same time, the demand from employers for graduates and better qualified school leavers will continue climbing, as the Institute of Manpower Studies pointed out in detail recently. Single employers like GEC/Marconi and the accountants Peat Marwick McLintock are now looking for 1,000 graduates a year out of a total output of 113,000.

The Higginson Committee evidently felt that it was in the business of finding a way to improve the participation rate in post-16 education as part of an overall policy for increasing the supply of graduates. Whether its proposals would have achieved this is doubtful. But whatever the merits of a five-subject curriculum, it is hard to find anybody who disagrees with the view that 'A' level in its current form actively deters many 16-year-olds from staying on in full-time education.

In order to appreciate fully the situation that now faces post-16 education, it is necessary to go back to the early 1980s and look at how the government responded to the first sharp increases in youth unemployment. The need to expand training facilities could have been met by restructuring and expanding post-16 education. It was the appropriate moment at which to introduce a qualification that did away with distinctions between one kind of education labelled vocational and another labelled academic. Accompanied by appropriate social policies, such a curriculum might have given Britain a fighting chance of matching the participation rates achieved abroad:

Country	In education until 18 (%)	Entering higher ed. (%)	Graduating (%)
USA	71.8	48.0	24.0
Japan	94.1	37.7	The majority
France	33.0	28.0	18.0
W. Germany	29.4	19.5	16.0
Britain	30.0	14.0	13.0

(Information as reported in the *Guardian* from the embassies of USA, Japan, W. Germany and France.)[2]

Instead, the decision was taken to establish a private sector in which 'Managing Agents', dependent upon MSC money, would be in direct competition with LEA provision. This represented a major assault on the status and authority of institutions that had sought to combine academic, general and vocational education under one roof. In future, it was quite clear, there would be a proliferation of organizations offering highly specialized courses. School sixth forms and sixth-form colleges could be fitted conveniently into this pattern as the providers of a specialized academic curriculum.

A selective system, even one that deploys the rhetoric of pupil and parent choice, will always be vulnerable to the reality of pupils' achievements and aspirations. The problem for the prospective students was one of sorting out the conflicting messages, the decision that YTS trainees would receive a 'wage' being typically ambiguous. While it clearly provided an incentive for leaving full-time education, it also suggested that vocational training was second best. Why else would it be necessary to offer inducements? As a consequence, large numbers of students ended up in the 'wrong' place and the education service was led down a path that actively disabled many school leavers from taking soundly based decisions about their future.

For reasons of this kind, post-16 education has continued to recruit students who may have acquired the right qualifications, but for whom a specialized academic education is probably inappropriate. Indeed, the mismatch between GCSE and 'A' level syllabuses may mean that the problem will become even more acute. Imagine, if you will, a group of students assembling for their first lesson in 'A' level English Literature after 2 years of GCSE. What will they be like? In principle, at least, they will be impatient with received wisdom, having learned that what matters is whether you have the ability to unravel problems and solve puzzles rather than parrot 'correct' answers. They will have discovered that it is more important to know how to reference resource material efficiently, than to commit facts to memory. In 'English' they will have experienced a much more varied diet of language than in the past, in which literature will have taken its place alongside other kinds of reading and writing. Ideally, the course they have followed should also have given them the confidence to voice their own 'response' not just to literature, but to all kinds of experience. By comparison with previous years, the messages about what counts as success at school will have been quite different.

Now set that against the HMI description of how 'A' level 'English Literature' is often taught:[3]

> ... there was still a considerable amount of teacher monologue in evidence, sometimes reading from inappropriate and old lecture notes. There was some dreary reading round the class, punctuated by glosses from the teacher. (A pembroke is a four-legged table, with flaps) and with no questions or discussion. There were narrow expositions on a variety of themes – the fool's character in 'King Lear', the theme of marriage in 'Emma', the nature of wit in metaphysical poetry, the historical detail of the battle of Agincourt where ideas were delivered at the pace of the slowest student's handwriting and students made either desultory or over-scrupulous notes according to temperament. Questions from the teacher were sometimes narrow or obscure, with a preconceived notion of the 'correct' answer, at which students aimed optimistic but erratic guesses. Some of the work which might have been close critical exegesis was little more than line by line paraphrase; a reading, for instance, of 'The Prelude' where the units of development within the poem were fractured by a

'translation' of each line which prevented a reading of the poem itself. Students were urged to 'know things inside out' – on several occasions – the chorus in 'Henry V', the chorus in 'Murder in the Cathedral', the order of Hamlet's soliloquies, the events of 'Emma' and the character of Mrs Morel. It was common for some teachers to re-word answers their students gave, in the interests, it was said, of giving the examiners what, on the evidence of close scrutiny of past papers, they were believed to want. Students often gave brief and hesitant answers and seemed afraid to err. Some of the teaching took place in the constant shadow of the examination with a narrow concentration on essay and context question to the exclusion of other activities, which had the effect of shrouding the vitality of literature in an air of gloomy retribution.

While it might reasonably be objected that what is being compared are best intentions for GCSE and worst practices at 'A' level, there can be no doubt about the scale of the problem. Even the most imaginative teachers of 'A' level English Literature are having to face difficult decisions about how to reconcile their previous practice with a completely new set of expectations.

Looking ahead

This combination of consumer demand for high-status courses, students unused to traditional academic disciplines, and a rapidly fragmenting subject, could prove unmanageable. Figure 9 is an attempt to show what might happen as the system struggles to come to terms with change. The key distinction it makes is between those alternatives that would follow from direct intervention by government, and those that would result from a decision to allow the system to evolve its own solutions.

In the absence of any policy direction from central government

The enthusiasm with which the syllabuses in 'Communication' and 'English Language' have been received, suggests that there remains a demand for new 'subjects'. One Examination Board has recently received a proposal for an 'A' level in 'Writing', and once categories of that kind are entertained the possibilities multiply. Television, Film or Media Studies all offer themselves as possible candidates, as well as Women's Studies and Popular Culture. More comparable with 'Writing' might be 'A' levels in, say, Documentary or 'The Oral Tradition'.

Courses with a vocational slant might include Journalism, Information Technology, Business English, and so on. The list could almost certainly be extended, and while some of the titles might seem fanciful, a convincing case could be made on behalf of almost all of them. The distinction between 'English Literature' and 'Writing', for example, is not much different from the distinction between 'Art' and 'History of Art', except that, by tradition, the orthodox course has been broadly academic and critical in one case, and broadly practical and creative in the other. 'Information Technology', to take another example, is beginning to feature quite frequently in the lower school curriculum (first to third years), and it is not unusual for the English Department to have become involved in teaching it.

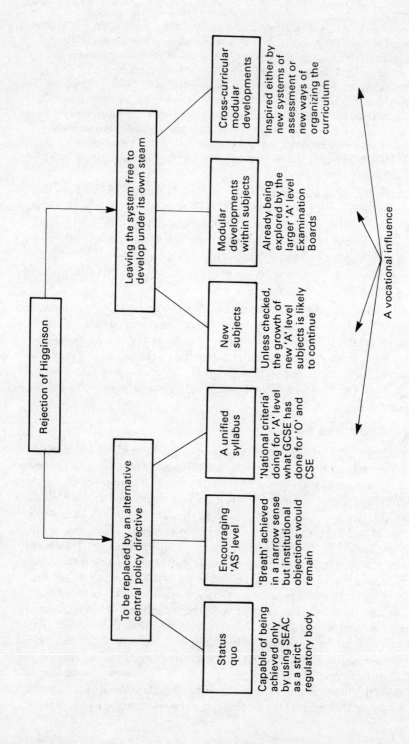

Figure 9

There are, however, powerful constraints on developments of this kind. The most obvious one is the Schools Examinations and Assessment Council (SEAC), which, as a good old-fashioned, regulatory body, would certainly wish to oversee change and to ensure some kind of continuity with existing provision. Less obvious, but equally influential, are the institutional constraints of small sixth forms. However desirable curriculum development might be, there is only a limited amount of room for manoeuvre. For both of these reasons, the number of new 'subjects' jostling for a place in the post-16 curriculum will probably be small. A pattern far more likely to develop is that of broad subject areas, as at present but including, say, 'English' and 'Media Studies', with a range of options on offer once you get inside.

There are plenty of precedents for a curriculum of this kind. The most flexible alternative is that of a 100 per cent course-work assessment which offers the teacher considerable autonomy within a general framework prescribed by the Examination Board. At the time of writing, a group of teachers based in the South of England are devising such a scheme for submission to the AEB. Whether it ever becomes widely available or not, it is unlikely to be the only or the final initiative of this kind. A more structured solution to the same problem is that of a syllabus based upon a menu of different options, either with or without a core element. At least two exam boards are considering proposals to restructure their existing provision in this way. Most progress has been made by the London Board which has developed further the pattern established when *Varieties of English* was made available as an alternative to the 'Unseen Criticism' paper. Into the melting pot have gone all the separately identifiable elements of their existing syllabuses ('Papers' in the jargon of ULSEB, whether they are assessed by final examination or not). Courses can be assembled by selecting the required elements, thereby allowing whatever mix of language and literature is thought desirable. The appropriate JMB committees have discussed a similar proposal that would make language and literature available within a common framework while extending the range of assessment to include open book examinations, and course work. New options could be incorporated into such a structure without radically altering the pattern of provision at 'A' level. Indeed this is exactly what is happening within a Modular 'A' level English Pilot being submitted to AEB as part of the 'Wessex Project'. An early draft of the proposal by Kevin Jeffery, the Co-ordinator for the pilot, describes a possible structure for the course,

> Structure: the course will be designed on the principle of 60% Core, 40% Extension Modules, in common with other schemes in the Wessex Project. The 40% modular element will be made up of 4 modules, chosen by the student from a bank available. These may be subject-based or inter-disciplinary (i.e. they will allow students to diversify into other areas of study compatible with their Core course, e.g. Theatre Arts, Language Study, Media Study, History, Mod. Languages, etc.).

The Core is based upon the two existing examination papers in AEB 660, the Board's alternative syllabus, whilst the modules 'would deliver the coursework component'. Some 'Ideas for Module Topics' are provided which, although only a set of titles, are very suggestive,

Intro. Module: induction course for new students – Storytelling
Genre-based: Poetry, the Novel, the short story, Travel writing
Period-based: 1st World War; the Victorians, Elizabethans, 60/70s
Movement: Romantics, Pre-Raphaelites, 'movement poets'
Culture-based: American, W. Indian, French, German writing
Lang. Study: Lang. acquisition, Lang. in Science/workplace
Media Study: Police/Young People/Education in the Media
Writing: Writing under the guidance of writer in resid.
Theory: History of Criticism, role of the reader.

They provide an interesting comparison with the CEE syllabus in 'Communication' established in the early seventies by the Southern Regional Examinations Board (SREB).[4] The course, which lasted a year, was composed of three modules taken from:

- *Literature modules:*

  Children's Literature
  Non-Fiction
  Popular Literature

- *Artists and their work/in any medium:*

  An Individual Artist and his Work
  The Study of a Particular Theme
  The Study of Work from a Particular Period

- *Drama modules:*

  Improvisation
  Group Activity towards a Workshop Production
  Study towards Production of a Play

- *Film modules:*

  Film Making and its Techniques
  Film from Books
  Film Appreciation and Study

- *The mass media:*

  A General Study
  A Specific Study

- *Language modules:*

  Language in Theory
  Language in Use
  Language Development of the Child

- *Organizations:*

  Communications in Organizations

- *The student's skills:*
  Speaking and Listening
  Writing
  Understanding
  Sense Perception

The title attached to the qualification that was finally awarded depended upon which of the 22 modules had been completed and offered for assessment. While it might once have seemed inconceivable that such a curriculum could provide a model for 'A' level, circumstances have changed. Since then, the 'alternative' syllabuses have provided a lot of experience about negotiating individual assignments and involving students in making decisions about their own work. What might have seemed a radical departure 15 years ago looks now like a possible solution to some otherwise intractable curriculum problems.

In response to policy

It is not easy to predict whether 'A' level will be left to develop in this kind of unregulated way. As it becomes increasingly unclear which syllabuses should be described as 'standard' and which as 'alternative', the government may decide to intervene. If it does, it will have a difficult job on its hands. As the Avon NATE proposals indicate, 'the way that new subjects have developed, with each new addition defining itself in distinct if not hostile opposition to its predecessors, has led to an arbitrary fragmentation of what might be better seen as a single field of study'. The problem is that where one person sees the solution somebody else sees another part of the problem. Both 'English Language' and, more controversially, 'Communication Studies' could also claim, at least in theory, to offer a framework for a 'single field of study'.

This difficulty is recognized by Avon NATE which is why Steve Bennison and Andrew Spicer describe their proposals as a 'dream syllabus' that 'may not be attractive to many teachers'. In practice, a single subject is not likely to be achieved by constructing a 'distinctive, coherent philosophy', however compelling that may be, but by a political intervention of the kind that led to GCSE.

The starting point for establishing 'national criteria' for an 'A' level English might well be something like the National Congress on Languages in Education (NCLE) report on *Language and Languages 16–19*. Drawing on the work of John Dixon and the Schools Council 16–19 English Project, the NCLE report argues that any analysis of post-16 education has to start from the 'curriculum distinction between academic and vocational purposes' which 'goes well beyond a matter merely of ideas'. The report offers a brief survey of the way in which this key distinction has become institutionalized:

> Traditions of universities, public examinations and schools have evolved separately from those of vocational qualifications, diplomas, apprenticeships and industrial training boards.

By starting from here it was possible for the report to argue that 'curricula of either an academic or vocational kind may be conceptualised as equally though differently specialised. This emphasis may be contrasted with broader social and personal and educational purposes.' The significance of this analysis is that it elbows the traditional academic curriculum away from the centre of the stage. Academic 'A' level courses cease to be the culmination of secondary education and become one option at 16.

The NCLE report adopted John Dixon's map, with some modifications, as a basis for its work (see Fig. 10). It is not difficult to identify where the two 'A' level Language syllabuses should appear. The London syllabus is firmly positioned underneath 'A' level Literature on the left-hand side, the JMB syllabus probably hovers somewhere between that and 'A' level Communications, with a foot in both camps.

In its recommendations, the NCLE report is understandably cautious. None the less, the message is quite clear:

> The intention to develop specialised uses of language does not preclude a basis in more general understandings about the role of language in society and in human affairs. More than this, we believe that the development of these understandings among teachers in the 16–19 sector provides a surer base for deepening practice than more and more specific course designs, syllabuses and materials.

What is significant about this is that it provides a way of acknowledging vocational needs as part of the mainstream curriculum. Raymond Williams (1983) puts it like this in *Culture and Society, 1780–1950*:

> There can be no adequate technical education which is not liberal and no liberal education which is not technical: that is, no education which does not impart both technique and intellectual vision. In simpler language, education should turn out the pupil with something he knows well and something he can do well. This intimate union of practice and theory aids both. The intellect does not work well in a vacuum.

What Williams makes clear is that the attempt to locate a syllabus in the middle ground where academic and vocational purposes meet is not some kind of flaccid

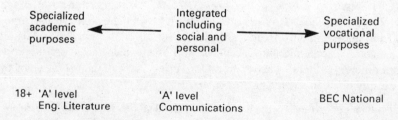

Figure 10   Curriculum, course and exam demands on language 16–19.

compromise. Nor is it a covert way of introducing a highly generalized curriculum suitable as a replacement for the 'universal truths' of the grammar school. On the contrary, it is part of the process by which the special status enjoyed by some kinds of discourse, and hence, curricula, is removed. Appendix C is a report produced by a group meeting at the annual conference of the National Association for Advisers in English (NAAE) who were attempting to sketch in the broad outlines of what such an integrated syllabus might look like.

A curriculum of this kind would bear comparison with the Australian Upper Secondary Curriculum as described in the Introduction. The similarities are, of course, no accident. What they demonstrate is that, given some agreement about the problem, there are only a limited number of solutions. Put less cryptically, this suggests that when teachers attempt to construct a curriculum capable of balancing a number of different demands, they will tend to reach for a concept of 'general' education, based upon skills that transcend particular versions of education, be they academic, vocational or personal.

That, of course, is what happened when the National Criteria were drawn up for GCSE. While there was no absolute requirement to reach consensus, the consultations that took place, and the criteria themselves, were clearly devised to ensure that no single view or sectional interest was favoured at the expense of any other. It is scarcely surprising that a rational attempt to sort out provision at 18+ should arrive at roughly similar conclusions.

It is hard to know whether the government will ever ask the question to which this kind of curriculum provides the answer. The concept of a 'general' education is based upon assumptions about equal access to educational opportunities that, in the late 1980s, are out of fashion. There is also a greater tolerance of direct political involvement in the curriculum than would once have been thought possible, and the government might choose to insist upon retaining the 'present character and rigorous standards'[5] of 'A' level by the simple expedient of outlawing experimentation. The problems that this would cause, of inappropriate provision and a high drop out rate, could well be politically less damaging than a decision to sanction reform.

Alternatives to alternatives

Whichever way you twist and turn in the attempt to find some kind of satisfactory curriculum package for English and related studies, the same difficulties recur. On the one hand, there are powerful arguments for redefining the subject in order to be less exclusive, and, on the other, there are almost irresistible pressures for greater specialization in the name of higher academic standards.

It is difficult to find any common ground without ditching the whole structure of a curriculum in which the building blocks are discrete subject areas. Putting together a timetable for an 'A' level student is a bit like winching into place a few huge pre-cast concrete structures. What is needed is something more flexible that encourages individual elements within a whole curriculum to illuminate each other and which allows students interested in, say, English literature, to choose something other than seven, eight or nine set books and a practical criticism paper. If such a scheme were to have credibility, it would probably need to be linked to a system of assessment that could continue to describe achievement in orthodox terms, by reference to subject expertise. But it is a mistake to think that the only way of arriving at a qualification in 'English' is to start a course called 'English'. It is not difficult to imagine programmes of study that might include elements of 'English' capable of being extracted for a final 'subject' assessment.

The attraction of such a cross-curricular arrangement is that it would make space within the curriculum to include more areas of study, while at the same time preserving a highly specific focus for the work. In place of a 'general' education based upon common, transferable skills, it would offer a way of assembling a diverse range of relatively narrow expertise. It would broaden the curriculum in a quite different way from that proposed by the Schools Council in the 1960s, providing an answer, for example, to the vexed question of how to include vocational work in the mainstream.

There is little point in working out the detail of such a proposal here. Suffice it to say that the curriculum would be, in the broadest sense, modular, and that it would require quite a sophisticated system of assessment. Perhaps the most readily available exemplar of how such a scheme might be constructed can be found in the Open University first degree system. It is possible to foresee a number of ways in which a curriculum of this kind might become established in schools and colleges. It is not out of the question that the examination boards might make the first moves. Ted Wragg[6] suggested in *The Guardian* that 'One way ahead might be to see the whole business in terms of units, where an AS level would become a single unit and an "A" level 2 units'. The pressure to devise discrete courses that make no claims to represent the coverage of an entire subject could offer real possibilities for change.

A different kind of solution might follow an increase in the amount of course-work assessment included in 'A' level syllabuses. There is no reason, other than caution, why a school or college should not dismantle all the 'A' levels it offers into a number of discrete elements, and reassemble them in whatever form it wishes, linking subjects, matching themes and encouraging connections. The importance of course-work assessment is that it would allow students (and teachers) to monitor progress through the range of courses on offer.

The modules in the Avon NATE syllabus suggest what kind of courses an institution might mount within the general curriculum area of the Arts and Humanities. A further illustration of what the content of such a curriculum might look like is provided by a recent AS submission made to JMB by the Institute for Irish Studies at Liverpool University – *The Identity of Ireland 1890–1926*.[7] Significantly, it was intended as a History syllabus, but it contains some genuinely novel and exciting proposals for work in 'English Literature'.

The Introduction to the syllabus immediately draws attention to the strengths of a multidisciplinary approach:

'The times are highly unfavourable for the cultivation of the intellectual faculties of Irishmen, save in the direction of devising means of resisting naked tyranny' (United Ireland, 1889).

This syllabus provides students with the opportunity to study the involvement of men and women of letters in a crucial period in the history of Ireland when part of the country gained independence from Britain. It examines the inter-play between Irish history and literature at a time when there were born and developed ideas of Irishness, of Ireland's relationship to England and to English culture, and of Ireland's past and its implications for Ireland's future. The approach combines a study of history and literature to explore why, how and with what effect, writers in Ireland sought to identify themselves with their community and to influence the way the community thought about itself.

The syllabus examines clearly defined aspects of the cultural and political life of Ireland in the late nineteenth and early twentieth centuries. Based upon selected works of prominent Irish writers who wrote in English, it explores the nature of Irish identity through the development of cultural nationalism and the notion of 'a fractured cultural tradition', the connection between the fall of Parnell and the rise of Irish literature, the Irish literary and Gaelic revivals, the Irish Literary Theatre, Roman Catholic middle class Ireland, and the character of the Irish revolution. Special consideration is given to Yeats, Joyce, O'Casey and Synge.

What is immediately striking about the syllabus is that it identifies the context within which writers such as those named in the final sentence were working. An example might help to stress the significance of this. An English sixth-former studying Yeats as an option within a conventional 'A' level Literature syllabus is likely to find his interest in Irish mythology charming but whimsical, almost eccentric. It will seem entirely literary, just 'subject matter'. That it was a genuine contribution to mainstream Irish politics, an important element in Irish nationalism, will seem almost inconceivable. The treatment of Yeats within this syllabus specifically identifies his 'importance in cultivating ideas of the heroic, mythical ideas of Cuchulain and the great age of Irish history; appropriation of these ideas by, and their influence on, the generation of the Easter Rising'. The literature begins to make sense because some explanation is available about why it was produced. It ceases to be a pastime, and becomes something rather more important. The history is similarly brought into focus because, in the words of one of the 'assessment objectives', candidates are required to formulate 'balanced judgements or conclusions based upon evidence which is at once "public" and "personal"'. The syllabus goes some way towards establishing historical and cultural understandings of how the individual personality is constituted.

This account has concentrated on the relationship between history and literature and, indeed, that is a central concern in the syllabus. The aims, for example, include 'understanding and knowledge of . . . the cultural and political context of literature'. It does, however, go beyond an exclusive preoccupation with literary texts, so that the personal study, for example, could 'draw upon a wide range of material, including works of literature, literary criticism, auto-biography, biography, cartoons, photographs, newspapers and magazines'. What this suggests is a unifying framework for language and literature of a kind that is missing in any of the existing syllabuses despite their attempts to allow schools to pick and mix from between Literature and Language 'A' levels.

Conclusion

There would be plenty of practical problems associated with any attempt to build a curriculum around elements of this kind. By and large, it has always been the case that where 'A' level has been reformed it has been in order to allow a more sophisticated pedagogy. The institution itself with its 'disciplinary boundaries' has remained intact. While the progress that has been made in allowing teachers to shift the emphasis from what is taught to what is learnt is substantial and important, it may not be enough. If 'English' in all its forms is to survive into the next century as a significant force within the curriculum, it may have to be reconstructed in quite radically different ways.

Appendices

Appendix A: Tom's Last Voyage

They put me into the caravan a few months ago. Them – the Social Services. Oh, don't get me wrong, I appreciate what they're trying to do, but some of the people working for them . . . well! They don't know what it is to be old. A caravan, at my age! Some fancy name for it too, I shouldn't wonder. Yes, saw it on the gate through the window of the bus as they drove me in:

'Experimental Independent Dwelling Units for Elderly Persons. Department of . . .' something or other. Independent Dwelling Units! Hah! Caravans. That's what they are – bloody caravans.

I'd been showed in. Make yourself comfortable. This is your home. Well, I looked around. Poky little place, it was – furnished and all, everything neat and tidy and clean and like no one had ever lived there. This wasn't a home. Still, that's a consolation. They haven't put me in a home. Money, see. They knew I had some, somewhere; and I don't tell them neither – there's life in you yet, Tom my old son. Don't let the buggers push you under.

Quiet at first, it was, quiet and nice – only some seagulls squealing, but I'm used to that – old sailor, you know. Merchant navy. I've been around, seen the world, what there is to see, people to meet, women to find and stay with for a while and enjoy and say goodbye and promise to write and leave and forget. Hundreds of ports, different places. Had a job remembering them all – some places I couldn't go ashore – too many bloody past admirers!

Still. I could've settled down. Family? None as such. Oh, a sister . . . Alice, in Brazil, or somewhere. She never writes. She's probably dead – climate does that. Most of my friends are dead. I don't recognise any names in the Deaths any more. Our generation has gone through.

As I say, it was quiet at first. Woman came in a van on the first night – 'Meals on Wheels' plastered in white letters on the side. She seemed nice – Ann. Anna? Something. I remember what she said to me:

'Now then Mr Croft. Time for dinner,' she said, sing-song. 'Eat it all up.' I ate it – fair enough, I suppose, you get used to your own cooking, and I never used to go out. Only Christmas, usually, to a pub. They're all young folk now though. Places are full. Of young folk.

There were some next door. Young folk, that is. Kids with a car, like a new toy. Woman in the van said the council'd let them stay in the old people's caravan till they got a house. Noisy sods. Woke me up in the middle of the night – driving round, shouting. I yelled at them, but they only laughed –

'Daft old twat! Now then, Grandad, why're you asleep in the middle of the afternoon?' Cheeky buggers. I pulled the curtains and went back to sleep. Middle of the afternoon my arse!

Little kids began coming a few weeks later – I mean little, not those yobbos next door. Shouldn't even be here. I decided to talk to the woman in the van about it. No, these kids came to see me, canny they were, nice kids. They used to come every few days. It began by one of them losing his ball under the caravan. They came up the cliff track on their bikes from the village – beach is too small to play football, town is too busy and too far away, I suppose.

I began to give them tea, biscuits – there was a shop quite near, I bought them there. They liked orange better than tea, so I got that instead. Even began drinking it myself!

Remember showing them photos; the ship, the crews I was with, snapshots of faraway places – all far away. I came to a last one, pulled it out from the musty pages – me, forty or fifty years ago, all dressed up.

'Who's this?' asked one little lad – Peter, I think he said. 'Who is it?'

'That's me, son. Years ago, mind.' A girl looked at me unconvinced.

'That's not you,' she said. 'You're old. The hair's different. Look.' She pointed it out. I told them that people change. They didn't understand, refused to believe the young man in the photo was me. They saw me as I was, as now, as I had always been, to them. Funny how kids steal your past – even that. It's all I had –

Oh God! Get out the violins and wipe the tear, baby dear, from your eye. The kids don't know. They're too young to understand age. That's your old decrepit mind wandering again, Tom my old son; you'll have to watch that, it's getting more frequent.

When the kids went I used to listen to the wireless. There's a television set in the caravan, but I never had one before and couldn't get used to them. I was listening to it – the wireless – one night (load of arty-farty rubbish was on) when someone knocked on the door. I looked through the curtains – a woman, youngish, standing in the rain outside. I opened the door and asked her what she wanted. Well, she said if I was the old man who bothered her kids I was to stop and I was to leave them alone and not worry them and that last night her little girl had come home crying about people turning white and creased and I was to stop telling them horror stories and shouldn't I know better than that what the hell did I think I was doing?

She stood there with the rain trickling down her flattened hair and the words streaming out of her mouth. I said nothing. She looked at me a second then turned and stalked off to a car on the road. I closed the door and sat down by the wireless. Some ponce was describing the mysteries of women. I didn't understand women – all they meant to me was a thing during shore-leave, like food and a decent kip and a floor that didn't move. This woman, could have been my daughter, grand-daughter! Talking to me like a naughty boy.

So they took my kids away and left me alone.

Only they never actually left me alone – morning, noon and bloody night with their television on or skidding the car around or shouting – those yobbos next door. I went to complain one night, in the early hours, they were playing records loud and noisy. They just gave me cheek, called me a 'poor old sod' and said I worked on 'a different time scale' or something, and ignored me. I tried to go back to sleep but the bloody racket was unbearable.

One day, I was having breakfast, another woman came, not the woman in the van (she stopped coming after a few weeks), another woman. Said she was a social worker or something like that. I let her in and immediately she began moving things about, 'tidying up', she said – interfering! I went over to stop her but must have knocked a cup because it fell and smashed. Maybe it was her dropped the cup. We looked at it for a moment then she began to clear it up. I think I was angry with her then, for breaking the cup, anyway she went away.

Next day, or some days later or maybe a week after, she was back. This time she came right in and sat down and began to talk, asking all sorts of nosey questions and writing it all down. Then she went away. I don't know what these council people are doing – let them get on with their business and leave me alone, eh Tom, leave me alone.

But she didn't. Week after week she was back, talking, questions, 'tidying up', interfering. One evening, she had just left. It was still light so I went to see the time, but my watch wasn't on my wrist. Well, I searched all my pockets – nothing – then I knew – she must have taken it. Stolen my watch! Bloody hell, I'd had that watch for years, engraved with my name and all, and she with her talking and questions had bloody well stolen it!

I lay all night raging to myself – just couldn't believe it. Anyway, about four or five in the morning she's back, knocking on the door. I reached for the jar where I kept my teeth, but that'd gone too. My God! The little bitch had stolen my teeth as well. I opened the door and yelled at her:

'What time do you call this, eh?' She looked blank and glanced at her watch. Her watch? She came in.

'Now then, Mr Croft. What's the matter now? Have you lost something?' – seeing me looking around. Two-faced bitch. I played along –

'Yes, my watch. And my . . . yes. My watch is missing.' Well, she said.

'Oh, well then come on. You and me can look for it together, can't we? We'll find your watch,' and she began to pretend looking for it, going into drawers, looking behind things. I stood and watched her. Then she put her hand on it.

'Here it is, all found!' – by the side of my bed. God knows how she slipped it back, pretending to look for it, pretending to find it. I went over and took it off the small bedside table. There too was the jar with my teeth in. She'd slipped those back too then, had she? I couldn't stand it no more, her looking at me.

'Out!' I yelled. 'Get out. Out. Go away! Leave me alone!' and I pushed her to the door and outside and slammed it shut, locked.

The next time was some time later. She brought a girl with her, so there were two of them. Said she was a student going with her on her rounds – oh aye. Two of them. Clever. Can't watch two of them, can I? That's four hands everywhere. Clever.

More questions, as a cover; both of them sat down, but I couldn't watch them both. When they'd gone I went through everything; drawers, cupboards, under the bed, in the bed. I emptied the fridge and checked everything to see what they'd stolen. But I couldn't remember what I had so I couldn't tell. Bitches! I left it all lying on the floor, and went to bed angry.

They came back later, though it was still light – maybe next day. Both of them – all innocent, like. I decided to face them.

'Well?' I said when they came in. 'What've you come for this time? Clock, watch again, money, clothes? What?' They didn't know what I meant; like Hell, they didn't!

'Now, now, Mr Croft. Calm yourself down,' she sang. That was it. The notebook came out – more bloody questions! I swore at them, and I rarely do that. They went, stepping over everything on the floor. I wondered what they had taken this time. They muttered together – they always muttered, so I couldn't hear them. They knew my hearing wasn't good, so they muttered. Conspiring together, moving aside some pans in the doorway, picking a tea-cloth from the steps, they went.

Another day. The days passed. I slept, listened to the wireless. I stopped going to the shop, too far away and I couldn't find my money. My razor'd gone too – someone stole it, I remember, but who? I didn't go out, so I didn't read the news. I got it on the wireless for a bit – news, that is – but the batteries ran out and I hadn't any more. So I didn't have it on again. Just as well – news is always so miserable, nowadays.

The bed was uncomfortable for a few nights till I found a plate and knife and fork under the sheets. Somebody had left them there. I put them with the others, in the sink, and later I put them away, but when I went back they were in the sink again and they'd been used. So I pushed a chair up against the door, to stop them getting in. I found some sticky tape, black electrician's tape, in a drawer on the floor, and I taped up the window locks. That ought to stop them getting in, I thought. I had some left so I used it on the fridge too. It was empty, but they'd steal anything. I sat in a gap on the bed and used to look at the sea out of the windows and look at my photographs and if you leaned back you couldn't see the land below you, the clifftop, only the sea, grey as it was, and it was like being on the bridge of a ship again but the horizon stayed still and you had to rock yourself, but that was alright because it didn't really matter it was just like a calm day somewhere near the equator, or just to the south, except, of course, that the sea was grey and not blue and the horizon stayed still and there were clouds in the sky but it didn't matter, it didn't matter at all and I stroked my bristly chin and stared out on the sea and wanted to go home, wherever that was, I wasn't sure, any more, isn't that funny?

One afternoon I woke up outside on the grass and they were there. They must have got in somehow and carried me out in my dressing-gown. My back was cold and wet and I looked up at them and asked them what the hell they were doing.

'Why, Mr Croft! What are you doing out here?' she said, looking down, and the other, the student, stood behind and looked on.

'Me? Why've you brought me out here?' I yelled, or maybe I just thought it, anyway she didn't answer but bent down to take my arm. Then I screamed out loud and couldn't believe it, the noise, and they, both of them, went away.

I wanted to get up out of the wet but they'd done something to me so I didn't. I sat there in my dressing-gown and I caught glimpses of twitching curtains in the other caravans but I thought.

'Bugger them! They're all the same; they're all together so bugger them!'

They came back, them, with two men, later. My voice had gone with the scream so I said nothing just glared at them they were all in it together, I knew. The men picked me up and she was mouthing words at me to make me think I was deaf, but I could hear the seagulls and so I knew. The men carried me to a van nearby that they had come in or maybe they had stolen it. Anyway, they put me in the back of the stolen van and the windows were darker on the outside than the inside – so no one would see what they were doing to me, I supposed.

The van started and they drove me onto the road and off we went, banging and clattering and round corners and the man who drove kept pressing his horn all the time so I couldn't hear a thing, not even the words that she was mouthing at me. I just glared at her.

Through the windows I could see we had come into the town away from the sea. We were going away from the sea and we slowed down and the van turned into a drive and up we went.

There was a sign outside in blue with white letters and it said something about old people but I didn't pay much attention. They took me inside and brought me to a little room and when I was dry I went down to see the other passengers.

The people here are nice – not the people who work here, them. The other passengers are all sensible people. They know what it is to be old because they're all old themselves and know what to talk about. Of course, I can't see the sea from my room, only trees in the park, so I sit in the big armchair and watch the kids playing football. Downstairs, they try to get old Tom to join them in silly games. But I won't play with them, not at my age, not at my time of life. I just like to watch the kids playing football and I've got all my old photos, except the one of me as a young man forty or fifty years ago all dressed up. I burnt that one. It wasn't real anyway, the little girl said so. Soon we'll be leaving the park and heading out into the open sea. It'll be good to get back out there after all these years. It's been a long time. Of course, we have all the provisions to get aboard yet. As soon as that's done we'll be off! I didn't think it were possible again, not at my time of life. They keep putting off the date we leave, but I know it'll be soon because a nice lady downstairs told me so.

'We all leave soon,' she said, and I agreed. So all I'm doing now is waiting and making last-minute preparations. That's the spirit, Tom my old son, don't let the buggers put you down!

Appendix B1: ULSEB English Language Studies 174

Aims

The syllabus in English Language Studies at Advanced level is intended to be relevant to a range of educational courses and career options. In its concern with the variety of forms and functions of the English Language, it offers preparation for courses with linguistic elements and for careers in which knowledge of and sensitivity to language will be required.

The aim is empirical investigation and description of English in use, both written and spoken, in which students will develop:

(a) an understanding of the forms and functions of English which makes explicit their intuitive knowledge of the language;
(b) some conceptual awareness of the systems underlying language and its use;
(c) sensitivity in their response to language and in their own use of English.

Assessment objectives

Candidates will be expected to demonstrate:

(a) some knowledge of the sound pattern, vocabulary and grammar of English and their relationships to meaning;
(b) understanding of historical, geographical and social features of variety and change in English;
(c) application of this knowledge and understanding to describe and analyse texts and transcripts of English, and to relate the linguistic features to function and context;
(d) the ability to describe some of the different features of written and spoken English, 'Standard English' and non-standard English, 'Received Pronunciation' and other accents;
(e) critical awareness of the differences between descriptive and prescriptive attitudes to language use;
(f) synthesis of their acquired knowledge and understanding to make general comment on English in use.

Content

The empirical study of English should be based on the descriptive analysis of texts and transcripts, examining the interrelated linguistic levels of phonology (sound pattern) or graphology (the writing system), lexis (vocabulary) and syntax (word and sentence structure) which combine to give meaning to a text or utterance in a context or situation. The investigation may include any spoken utterance or written text in English, but the following important and interesting aspects of the language are recommended as areas for investigation:

written and spoken accounts of the same topic or event;
dialectal and standard English, both regionally and socially situated, and English outside the British Isles;
children's and adults' speech;

the media – newspaper and magazine styles and content, radio and television; literary
  texts;
the historical dimension – texts of different periods, in original spelling where possible;
the English of ethnic groups;
conversation and discourse;
pidgins and creoles derived from English;
'the language of . . .' – style related to event and situation, e.g. legal language,
  unscripted commentary, advertising, religious services, teachers to pupils / pupils to
  teachers / pupils to pupils, social sub-groups, bureaucracy . . .

The language of the students' own environment – spoken and written, at school or college,
at home and in the neighbourhood – will provide an immediate rich source of data for
discussion, analysis and evaluation. The acquisition of skills in phonological, lexical and
syntactic analysis should proceed concurrently with the study of texts and transcripts. The
following indicate the concepts and categories to be covered in broad terms:

Spoken and written English
Spoken English: the vowels and consonants of Received Pronunciation, in comparison
with those of local pronunciation; syllable and stress in words; rhythm and intonation of
utterances; assimilation and elision in ordinary speech; normal non-fluency and performance features of speech – hesitation, self-correction, fillers; paralinguistic features of
communication accompanying speech, both vocal and non-vocal; discourse – formal and
informal situations, speech act, conversational analysis.

Written English: the Roman alphabet in relation to the sounds of English; conventions of
the spelling system and punctuation.

Speech and writing: contrasted media for language – differing in acquisition, operation
and use, grammar, style and cohesion; the written sentence in relation to the spoken
utterance.

Varieties of English
Dialects and accents: differences of pronunciation, with reference to RP as a norm;
differences of vocabulary, word-inflection and grammar, with reference to Standard
English; the relationship of these differences to regional and social variation in urban and
rural environments.

Style in speech and writing: the appropriate use of language in a situation with reference to
the participants and their relative status, the medium of communication, the topic of
discourse, and the setting – including the occasion and the place; modality, tone, point of
view; stylistic features – including prominence, foregrounding, phonological patterning –
metre, rhyme, alliteration, assonance, syntactic patterning – parallelism, periodic and
loose sentence structure; content and expression – ambiguity; irony, simile, metaphor,
metonymy; implied author and implied reader in literature.

Historical change: differences between contemporary and earlier forms of English in
terms of spelling (with some reference to major changes in pronunciation), vocabulary
(contrasting Germanic word stock with French, Latin and other loans in terms of gains
and losses), the loss of word inflections, and changes in word order; contemporary dialects
of English as a source of older or alternative historical forms of word and structure.

Attitudes to contemporary usage: the prescriptive and descriptive approaches to language use – with reference to such notions as appropriateness, acceptability, grammaticality and correctness.

Terminology will provide students with the tools of analysis and the means of conveying their perceptions. There is no standard terminology, and any consistent use of recognised linguistic or stylistic terms by candidates will be acceptable. The following selected list of terms is provided as a guide only:

General: language, dialect, accent, idiolect, standard, non-standard; formal, informal, slang, jargon.

Spoken English: vowel, diphthong, consonant; syllable, rhythm, intonation.

Written English: alphabet, letter, digraph, spelling, punctuation.

Vocabulary and word meaning: affix, prefix, suffix, inflection, compound; word class (part of speech), lexical and function words, homonym, synonym, antonym, denotative, connotative, semantic features; collocation, idiom.

Syntax: sentence, clause, phrase and word structure; gender, number (singular, plural), count/non-count, case, person, tense, aspect, voice; co-ordination, subordination, complementation, embedding; subject, verb, object, complement, adjunct; declarative, interrogative, negative, imperative/statement, question, request, negation, command; cohesion – including reference, substitution, ellipsis, collocation.

The examination

Candidates will be required to take two examination papers of three hours each and to submit a project of not more than 3,000 words before the final examination. The two examination papers and the project will each carry one third of the subject marks.

Paper 2: Varieties of English
An examination paper providing a choice of written texts and transcripts for analysis and description.

Paper 5: Aspects of English
An examination paper with a choice of topics to cover the syllabus Content. Candidates will be required to answer questions based on textual material or data and on particular topics, including an 'editorial' question to assess their own writing.

Paper 6: The spoken language
A project on a specific area of the spoken language based on transcription and analysis, to be assessed by the Board's examiners.
 The completed project must be available for assessment by **1 May** for the June examination, and by the beginning of the examination period in January for the January examination. (Separate instructions will be issued for the submission of the project for the Board's assessment.)

Syllabus

Paper 2: Varieties of English
The aim of this paper is the description of, and commentary on, samples of English. Candidates will be required to answer *two* questions, with a choice, on passages of English which may include transcripts of speech and extracts from both literary and non-literary texts. They will be expected to make simple descriptive analyses of single texts, or contrastive analyses of two or more texts, in order to relate the linguistic features to the functions and contexts of situation and to show their awareness and understanding of the nature of language variety and change of the factors affecting the styles and uses of English.

Paper 5: Aspects of English
This paper will invite candidates to write more reflectively on aspects of language observation and analysis and on attitudes to English in use, in the terms of the concepts and categories indicated in the syllabus Content. They will also be required to demonstrate their own writing skills in an 'editorial' task based on textual material. The paper will be in three sections and candidates will be required to answer *three* questions, one from each section. Section A will consist of 'editorial' tasks of different kinds – adaptation or rewriting of material in various ways, or writing in response to given material – with commentary on the 'editorial' processes involved. Section B will consist of questions based on textual material and data requiring commentary and generalisation of various kinds, not necessarily in essay form. Section C will consist of essay questions on particular topics.

Paper 6: The spoken language – Project
The project provides an opportunity for candidates to make a practical study of the spoken language in a specific context. The project is to be based on a study of recorded speech and should include the transcription of 3–5 minutes of recorded material. Candidates should record their own material, but they should bear in mind that both recording and transcribing may involve considerable periods of time. Since transcribing conversation makes greater demands than transcribing solo narrative, 3–4 minutes of conversation should normally be sufficient, whereas 4–5 minutes of solo narrative may be appropriate. Ordinary spelling should normally be used for the transcription, but candidates should indicate clearly any conventions used for marking aspects of speech such as stress and intonation, pauses and hesitations. Phonemic or phonetic transcriptions, using the symbols of the International Phonetic Association, may be included as part of the transcription and may also be used in the accompanying commentary.

Candidates will be expected to comment on the implications of the chosen area of the spoken language and to discuss interesting and significant features of the recorded material on which the project is based, with particular reference to a selective description of sounds and/or forms of the material transcribed. The project should normally take the following general form:

(a) Introduction – a general discussion of the area of the spoken language chosen for study, indicating the focus of interest and the approach adopted;
(b) Description – a general account of the recorded material on which the study is based, indicating its source and giving any appropriate background information;

(c) Transcription – a complete transcription of 3–5 minutes of the recorded material, comprising a single continuous passage or several extracts;

(d) Analysis – a selective description of interesting and significant features of sound and/or form in the material transcribed, with reference as appropriate to features in the rest of the recorded material;

(e) Evaluation – a commentary on the insights afforded by the analysis and on the findings of the whole study.

The length of the project should not normally exceed 3,000 words; the transcription (c) of 3–5 minutes of the recorded material is additional to this. The project will be assessed for a clear focus to the study, an adequate transcription, an effective analysis and an informative commentary. The project will also be assessed for its appropriateness and effectiveness as a written report of a study. It is essential that the project is based on a manageable area of study, involving a small but productive amount of material. The following are typical of areas of study that could be considered:

> conversation analysis;
> the language of the young pre-school child;
> sales talk (between customer and salesman), e.g. in shop or market or on the door step;
> radio talk, e.g. disc-jockey, sports commentary, interview, phone-in, news item.

The cassette recording of the transcribed material must accompany the project on submission for assessment, according to the instructions to be issued by the Board. The cassette will not be assessed but may be used by the examiner in assessing the transcription and commentary in the project, and the recording should be of an acceptable sound quality. If more than the transcribed material is included on the cassette the sections transcribed must be clearly indicated on the cassette contents card in terms of minutes and seconds of tape time.

Notes for guidance

The following series of text-books, Studies in English Language, is suggested for reading and classroom use:

D. Freeborn – P. French – D. Langford, Varieties of English: an introduction to the study of language (+ cassette tape, Macmillan); D. Freeborn, A Course Book in English Grammar (Macmillan); P. French, Spoken English (+ cassette tape, Macmillan); D. Langford, Analysing Talk (+ cassette tape, Macmillan). W. R. O'Donnell – L. Todd, Variety in Contemporary English (Allen & Unwin); R. Quirk, The Use of English (Longman); G. Brown, Listening to Spoken English (Longman); M. Wakelin, Discovering English Dialects (Shire Publications); D. Crystal & D. Davy, Investigating English Style (Longman); A. Cluysenaar, Introduction to Literary Stylistics (Batsford); D. Crystal, What is Linguistics? (Arnold); D. Leith, A Social History of English (Routledge & Kegan Paul).

A detailed list of further reading suggested for teachers is available on request.

Paper 2, 'Varieties of English' is also available in the alternative syllabuses in **English** *at Advanced level (Subject numbers* **175** *and* **176***) given on page 210.*

Appendix B2: JMB English Language (Advanced)

English Language (Advanced) (two written papers each of three hours and the internal assessment of a set of original writing and a project on language use).

Centres wishing to enter candidates for this syllabus must write to the Secretary, at least two years prior to the Summer Examination in which the candidates will be presented for certification, requesting further details of the syllabus in order that they can give full consideration to the procedures involved and be allocated to an appropriate regional group.

A. The aims of the syllabus

The syllabus has been designed to enable centres to provide a course in the study of language with particular reference to the uses of spoken and written English. It aims to combine learning about the nature and functions of language in human thought and communication with learning how to use English more effectively. Students are introduced to a more systematic study of the English language than may have been encountered at O-level and are required to demonstrate more advanced expertise in a variety of language uses.

B. The objectives of the examination

The examination has been designed to assess the following:

(a) intellectual understanding in specified areas of theoretical knowledge about language and its uses;
(b) critical responses to a variety of language material;
(c) interpretative abilities in comprehending, adapting and re-presenting source material;
(d) investigative abilities in undertaking and reporting a small-scale study of an aspect of language in everyday use;
(e) imaginativeness and judgement in producing original work for a variety of specified purposes and audiences.

C. The form of the examination

Paper I (three hours) (30 per cent) in which candidates must answer one question from each of three sections. The paper will always cover the syllabus content as identified in Section F but there may be minor variations in the style of questions set.

Section A will contain a choice of essay questions inviting the candidate to discuss theoretical issues about the nature and functions of language. (10 per cent) (In their response to this section candidates must not substantially repeat material which has been used in the project.)

Section B will require candidates to respond critically to selected examples of literary material. Examples of prose and verse will be offered; candidates may opt for either. (10 per cent)

Section C will require candidates to respond critically to selected examples of non-literary material. (10 per cent)

Paper II (three hours) (30 per cent) This is a case study paper.

The questions will be made known to the candidate only at the time of the examination but source material, upon which the questions will be based, will be given to the candidate 48 hours before the examination. The source material is provided in advance of the examination to enable candidates to familiarize themselves with each collection of source material and, therefore, enable them to make their choice of question in the examination with the minimum of delay. Candidates will be expected to read *three* varied sets of source material but will be required to answer only *one question on one set of material* at the time of the examination. There must be no prior discussion of the source material between teacher and candidate and candidates must bring only the source material with them to the examination. Questions will be in the form of tasks inviting candidates to interpret, adapt and re-present source material for specified purposes and audiences other than those originally intended.

Course work (40 per cent)

(a) *three original pieces of writing* appropriate to different audiences, purposes and contexts accompanied by a commentary. (See syllabus page 4 paragraph (d) and Instructions and guidance for teachers.) (20 per cent)

Candidates should produce between 3500–5000 words, including at least one substantial piece but excluding commentary. (See Instructions and guidance paragraph 12.)

A taped presentation would be an acceptable alternative to one written piece.

(b) *one project* reporting an investigation into a chosen aspect of language use (2000 to 4000 words). (20 per cent)

(Candidates must not substantially repeat in Section A of Paper I material which has been used in the project.)

D. Assessment

Paper I and Paper II will be set and marked by the Board's examiners.

The three original pieces of writing and the project will be internally assessed by the teachers at the centre. Each centre's assessments will be moderated by the Regional Group Moderator appointed by the Board.

E. Supervision and authentication of course work

The course work must be prepared, supervised and assessed in accordance with the Instructions and guidance for teachers on internal assessment of original writing and project in English Language (Advanced), copies of which must be obtained from the Secretary at the beginning of the course. This pamphlet contains advice on the requirements of the course work, details of standardisation and moderation procedures and criteria for assessment.

It is essential that all candidates and staff concerned are aware that under the Joint Matriculation Board's GCE Regulations candidates are forbidden to indulge in any unfair practice in the carrying out of course work submitted for assessment as part of the examination. Candidates will be required to certify, when submitting their course work to the assessing teacher that they have been made aware of the regulations relating to unfair practice and that the submission is their own unaided work.

Any candidate who uses, or is suspected of using or attempting to use, any unfair means is to be reported immediately to the Secretary. If the Board is satisfied that an offence has been committed, the candidate will be liable to be disqualified in all the subjects offered in the current examination for the General Certificate of Education, including all work completed before and after the offence was committed.

It is appreciated that a piece of course work could involve a candidate in searching for and using information assembled by others and in considering conclusions drawn by others on a particular topic. There is nevertheless an important distinction between the improper use of copied material and the acquisition of information obtained by research; the distinction lies in the use made by the candidate of the information obtained and the extent to which the sources of information are acknowledged. The candidate must give details of any source used in the preparation of course work. All direct quotations must be indicated by means of quotation marks and the sources given.

The signing by the staff of the centre of the record cards and results cards involves the guarantee that 'every step has been taken to ensure that the assignments submitted are the work of the candidate concerned'.

The Head of the centre will also be required to endorse the teacher's declarations. Before entering candidates for English Language (Advanced) the centre should give careful consideration to the requirements and ensure that the allocation of staff time and resources is such that all the requirements can be met. A considerable amount of individual attention needs to be given to each student at all stages of preparation of the project and the folder of original writing.

The standardisation and moderation procedures for the course work component of English Language (Advanced) require that participating centres reach an acceptable measure of agreement about standards. For this purpose centres are organised into regional groups. Teachers who are to be responsible for the assessment of candidates are required to participate in group agreement trials. Samples of original writing and project work from the previous year's examinations, selected and graded by the Moderators in conjunction with the Chairman of Examiners, are assessed by participating teachers in advance of the agreement trial meeting. The resulting assessments are discussed at the meeting. There are normally two agreement trials per academic year.

F. Content of the syllabus

The syllabus requires a basic knowledge of the elements of linguistic description which will enable candidates adequately and appropriately to apply that knowledge accurately to all relevant areas of the syllabus.

(a) *Theoretical knowledge about the nature and functions of language* (Paper I)

The essential elements in this area are an understanding of the nature and functions of language and a systematic study of the structure of English in terms of its phonology, grammar and semantics.

Language study has relationships with other disciplines, such as sociology, psychology, philosophy, anthropology and literary criticism. Candidates will be expected to apply their basic knowledge of linguistic description to at least *one* of the following topics:

  (i) Language and society.
 (ii) Language acquisition.
(iii) Language varieties.
(iv) Language change.

(b) *Critical responses to varieties of language use* (Paper I)

   This section of the syllabus is primarily concerned with the ability to describe and assess the demands made by a variety of texts and to articulate critical responses. Criticism should be informed by knowledge of the forms and conventions of written English and show an awareness of the importance of purpose, context and register for reading comprehension and for communication.

   Whereas the A level literature syllabus is concerned exclusively with literary texts in English, equal attention is given in the language syllabus to non-literary material. This should include persuasive, instructional and informative forms of contemporary writing. Particular attention should be paid to relationships between the style and the content of material and to the ways in which both intended and unintended meanings and effects are conveyed.

(c) *Interpretative uses of language* (Paper II)

   This section of the syllabus should give students the experience of interpreting, adapting, editing and re-presenting source material to audiences other than those originally intended. Work undertaken will be to some extent dependent upon reading abilities developed in section (b) of the syllabus but should be guided by a study of different modes of interpretation and editorial presentation e.g.

  (i) TV, Film, Radio or Play scripts of a documentary or semi-documentary nature.
 (ii) Technical reports and reviews.
(iii) Social reports and surveys.
(iv) Business writing (e.g. minutes, memoranda, agenda reports).
 (v) Anthologies or collections with annotations and commentary.
(vi) Biography and History writing.

(d) *Candidates' own writing* (Course work (a) Original Writing)

   This section of the syllabus is concerned with candidates' own performance as language users. They will be expected to have undertaken a critical evaluation of their own writing and this should be incorporated into a commentary supplied with the pieces of writing along with earlier drafts.

   Candidates will be expected to produce three different kinds of writing. The range of possible kinds includes writing which entertains, persuades, informs or instructs.

(e) *Investigation into language use* (Course work (b) The Project)

   This section of the syllabus requires candidates to report on a personal investigation into a specified aspect of language use in everyday life using the knowledge acquired in (a) (Theoretical Knowledge about the Nature and Functions of Language). Topics are to be chosen and closely defined by students after careful consultation with their teachers. Any topic which teachers judge to be appropriate to the course – and to the abilities and interests of their students – may be attempted. Sample topic areas are included below. Teachers who are uncertain of the viability of a particular area of research are advised to contact the Board. Centres entering candidates for the first time must submit topic titles for approval by the Project Moderator not later than 1 October in the year of the examination. Some indication of potential problems which may be encountered by students undertaking research on particular areas is given in the Instructions and guidance for teachers.

Suggested topic areas

(i) An analytical study of some differences between spoken and written English (e.g. radio vs. press news, or sports reports).

(ii) A study of transcribed examples of a regional variety of spoken English. (Students may wish to make a detailed study of phonological features, or to attempt a broader analysis of a variety of features, including those of lexis and grammar as well as phonology.)

(iii) A study of examples of the English spelling system (e.g. as exemplified in spelling problems encountered by young children).

(iv) Observations of the speech (or writing) of individuals in the process of language development. Students may wish to concentrate on the language of young children during the early stages of development, or to study that of adults (e.g. in an EFL or ESL class).

(v) A study of norms and variations in everyday uses of English (e.g. making requests, giving instructions, greetings).

(vi) A transcription (with commentary) of a stretch of everyday discourse (e.g. family talk; committee meeting; argument).

(vii) A description of some characteristics of the written and/or spoken English of a distinct occupational, professional or other social group (e.g. lawyers, doctors, the police, the courts, politicians).

(viii) An exploration of stylistic features of popular media (e.g. a contrast between features in publications with different political persuasions; song lyrics in the 1940s and 1980s on a common theme; the language of TV programmes designed for children of different ages; the language of teenage magazines compared with those marketed for adults; the language of adverts aimed at different audiences).

(ix) An analysis and comparison of contrasted texts (e.g. a nineteenth century auto-biography and a contemporary autobiography, a text book on English from the 1930s and one from the 1980s, extracts from two novels describing a particular experience from different viewpoints, two different story books written for children).

(x) A study of language choices made by bi- or multi-lingual individuals in the community (e.g. factors triggering language choice for speakers of Panjabi, Urdu and English, or Jamaican Creole and English).

(xi) An exploration of some features of a particular language in use in the community, compared with English (e.g. comparison of the grammatical structures of Panjabi or Jamaican Creole with those of English).

(xii) An analysis of a particular area of semantics in English (e.g. the operation of metaphor in everyday uses of English, study of historical development and contemporary uses of certain lexical items).

(f) *Recommended texts*

The syllabus does not prescribe specific texts for study but a list of suggestions for reading has been prepared for the benefit of centres and is available from the Secretary. The list is not exhaustive and the appearance of a book on the list cannot guarantee that the book will remain in print.

G. Conditions which apply to centres entering candidates for English Language (Advanced)

(a) Teachers who are to be responsible for course work assessments must participate in agreement trials.

(b) Centres wishing to take part in English Language (Advanced) must be in a position to join a suitable group of centres for the purpose of agreement trial meetings. The operation of the course work scheme of moderation is dependent upon there being a sufficient number of participating centres within a reasonably compact geographical area. It is recognised that variations may be appropriate in rural areas. The Board will take such factors into account in determining the composition of groups.

(c) The travelling expenses of those attending group trial marking meetings are *not* paid by the Board although a nominal fee is paid to the staff of centres for each candidate assessed.

(d) The Board reserves the right to withhold or withdraw approval of the entry of candidates from any centre.

(e) Centres will be expected to provide from among their participating teachers, persons willing in principle to undertake the duties of Group Chairman and Group Secretary.

(f) Entries from external candidates cannot be accepted for this form of assessment.

(g) Centres wishing to enter candidates for English Language (Advanced) must write to the Secretary, at least two years prior to the Summer Examination in which the candidates will be presented for certification, requesting further details of the syllabus in order that they can give full consideration to the procedures involved and be allocated to an appropriate regional group.

Appendix B3: AEB Communication Studies, Advanced Level (608)

Revised syllabus for first examination in June 1986 (two papers, each of three hours, a project and an oral test)

1. Aims

The aim of the syllabus is to promote knowledge of, understanding of, and competence in communication by:

1.1 study of categories, forms and uses of communication, in order to interpret major theories and issues;
1.2 application of this study to *cases* drawn from authentic situations;
1.3 development of practical skills in communication.

2. Objectives

The successful candidate will be able to demonstrate knowledge, understanding, and skills in the three areas of activity described under the 'aim of the syllabus' above, by:

2.1 showing knowledge and understanding of major theories of intrapersonal, interpersonal, group, mass and extrapersonal communication; (1.1)
2.2 showing knowledge and understanding of major contemporary political, economic and social issues in communication; (1.1)
2.3 showing knowledge and understanding of the interaction between people and machines and of current or potential development in communication technology; (1.1)
2.4 offering description and interpretation of communication in a given context; (1.2)
2.5 playing a communication role or roles in a given context or contexts; (1.2)
2.6 applying relevant theories to cases; (1.2)
2.7 applying understanding of issues to cases; (1.2)
2.8 demonstrating, through case studies (paper 2) and the project (paper 3), the ability to use communication skills and techniques accurately and appropriately in a wide range of means of communication; (1.2/1.3)
2.9 using these skills and techniques to show awareness of factors which influence the communication process. (1.3)

3. Examination structure

Two three-hour papers, externally examined, plus a project, which will be internally examined, and Board moderated. Paper 1 will receive 40% of the total marks. Papers 2 and 3 will each receive 30% of the total marks.

3.1 *Paper 1*
There will be two sections, A and B. Four questions are to be answered, one of which will be from Section A, and three from Section B.

A variety of forms of communication may be offered for some questions.

Graphic and diagrammatic responses may be required, as well as the standard essay, or a number of short answers.

3.2 *Paper 2 – Case study*

One or two Case Studies may be offered. If only one Case Study is offered, candidates will be given a choice of roles and tasks.

Questions will test the ability to adapt theories and/or models to practical situations, to adopt a mode or modes of communication appropriate to a particular role or roles, and to evaluate the case study materials.

3.3 *Paper 3 – Project*

20% of the total examination marks will be awarded for the work, the diary/log, and for written assessment by the candidate.

10% of the total examination marks will be awarded for a short individual oral presentation relating to the project work and its creation, and for effective participation in a subsequent group discussion.

The project must be original in execution, if not in source material.

It must be in an acceptable form which demonstrates competence in achieving the objectives stated above.

4. Syllabus

The syllabus describes subjects of enquiry and practice. These areas should be seen as contributing collectively to the study of the communication process a range of possible situations.

4.1 *Categories of communication*

Guidance Notes

4.1.1 Intrapersonal Communication: the study of the communication process within the individual, and as it relates to other categories.

Includes concepts such as self-image, self-esteem, and the processes of perception, cognition and the generation of meanings.

4.1.2 Interpersonal Communication: including the study of dyadic communication, and factors affecting this process in a wide range of situations.

Includes such factors as perception, culture, experience performance, self-presentation.

4.1.3 Extrapersonal Communication: including communication through and to non-human and inanimate sources and resources.

Includes the nature of communication between people and machines, including the development of machine intelligence.

4.1.4 Group Communication: including distinctions between large and small groups; formal and informal groups; ways in which communication is used by groups within themselves and with others; communication

Includes ways in which formal and informal groups use communication to achieve goals, reinforce norms, and display identity. Study of institutions includes the handling of information and decision-making, and the problems of within and between institutions.

maintaining effective communication within and between large groups.

4.1.5 Mass Communication: including study of the mass media and of the institutions, characteristics, and effects of kinds of mass communication.

Includes such mass media as radio, television and the press and such concepts as access, control, audience, mediation and stereotyping.

4.2 *Forms of communication*

4.2.1 Oral communication.

Includes individual presentation; types of two-way exchange (for example, interviews); types of discussion (for example, debates); recognition of paralinguistic features (for example, tone and intonation, accent, stress).

4.2.2 Written and printed communication.

Includes texts in a wide variety of styles and registers.

4.2.3 Non-Verbal communication.

Includes the effects and uses of body language, dress and display cues. Recognition of its importance for communicating roles, attitudes and emotions.

4.2.4 Graphical communication.

Includes graphics in their pictorial and symbolic modes; analysis of ways (including conventions) by which images are constructed, as well as sequences of images (visual narrative).

4.2.5 Numerical communication.

Includes the application and significance of systems of number, and the presentation and interpretation of data in numerical form.

4.2.6 New technologies.

Includes appreciation of the uses and effects of communication technologies; information technology; the personal and social implications of new technologies. Opportunities are provided for detailed technical knowledge to be used as, for example, in computer studies.

4.3 *Use of communication*

4.3.1 Information gathering, storage, retrieval, dissemination.

Includes definitions of the term 'information'; kinds of public access to information sources; ways of expressing information through various media; the processing of information by institutions, kinds of power conferred by possession, control and marketing of information.

4.3.2 Persuasion, propaganda and publicity.

Includes study of their purposes and their effects on individual or audience in interpersonal as well as mass communication contexts.

4.3.3 Entertainment.

Includes study of audience activity/passivity; the difference between consuming entertainment and making it; the marketing of communication as a commodity; cultural implications; interaction between the media in generating entertainment.

4.3.4 Socialisation.

Includes the production of values through communication; the reinforcement of norm in groups and institutions; the acquisition of individual roles; the integration of individual into social groups; the part communication plays in constructing social reality; political awareness and activity.

4.3.5 Social Functioning.

Includes study of expressive and affiliated needs, and personal growth, relating particularly to the categories of interpersonal and group communication; creative expression in the arts.

4.4 *Theory in Communication Studies*

4.4.1 Identification of basic factors; description of principles; discussion of hypotheses; uses and limitations of models.

Area of study includes theories presented within the four divisions described, for example the concept of need operating a factor across a range of communication situations (Berlo); the principle that context of reception always affects understanding of communication (Schramm); hypothesis that communication may be understood as an instrument of control (Smith); the 'advocacy' model as a means of understanding how politics are mediated through television (Tracey).

It should be made clear that in respect of models in particular, criticism of existing models is to be encouraged, as is the production of original models.

4.4.2 Description and interpretation of the communication process in a variety of situations.

4.4.3 Description and interpretation of the development of mass communications from the late nineteenth century and of the significance of this for contemporary society, and for the future.

4.5 *Issues in Communication Studies*

Description and discussion of those issues raised by communications activity within political, economic, social, and cultural spheres.

Issues in communication studies are public debates of an ethical, moral, political, or social nature that are defined by agencies such as the media, the education system, and organs of public discussion. (Examples include the question of control of and access to electronic means of information storage and questions relating to the production of gender stereotypes through the media.) Particular reference will be made to those issues concerned with the organisation, functioning, and effects of mass communication; as well as to those issues relating to the impact of technology on communication experienced by the individual and by society as a whole.

Appendix C: NAAE Conference 1988, English 16–19

1. Background

The aim that the group set itself was to find some kind of unifying structure for the variety of 'A' level syllabuses currently available in the broad area of 'English Studies'. The best known of these syllabuses are 'Communications Studies', 'English Language' and the various conventional and 'alternative' syllabuses now on offer as 'A' level English Literature. Taken together, they represent a much broader concept of what 'English 16–19' might be than has traditionally been available from examination boards, and one that is much more appropriate for students who have been following GCSE courses pre-16.

It is difficult to say whether the attempt to compress so many syllabuses into one has any real significance beyond its value as a focus for discussion about the 16–19 curriculum. Something similar has been attempted by the Avon NATE branch in the proposals recently published in the 'English Magazine', and reactions at the conference made clear that it would not be easy to gather a consensus, even within the profession, for any single interpretation of what 'English 16–19' ought to be. Once it is acknowledged that there are wider political, social and institutional pressures standing in the way of agreement, the task may seem a futile one. For what it is worth, however, here is another attempt that, despite being sketchy in the extreme, might stand alongside the Avon proposals as a basis for further discussion.

2. A structure

It was felt that recent thinking about the modular curriculum offered the best way of balancing both breadth and depth in 'A' level English. The 'Higginson' report stresses that

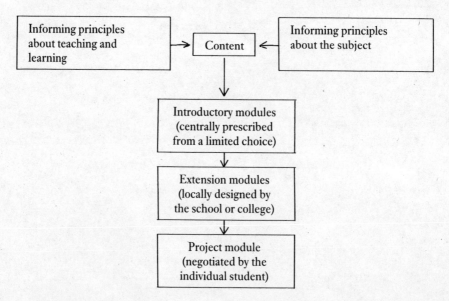

the two are not mutually exclusive and the pattern that was finally established rests upon this assumption; a breadth of understanding is what makes possible a depth of perception. Two characteristics of the final scheme deserve some brief comment. The 'Informing Principles' are explicitly stated in order to highlight the spirit of the scheme. Had there been time to work in greater detail, it would have been in accordance with these principles. Secondly, the modules should not be viewed as inflexible or watertight. During the course of the discussion they became less and less prescriptive – more a way of constructing a syllabus with optional elements, than of determining a sequence of lessons. The final section of this report includes some speculative observations about the scheme in action.

2.1. *Informing principles about teaching and learning*
It is intended that these principles should inform both the structure of the course (construction of modules) and the pedagogy adopted in the classroom.

A. Students should be encouraged to become independent, autonomous and active learners.

  COMMENT: There is no single way of achieving an outcome of this kind. Different models of learning can be proposed, as, for example,

  Survey
  ↓
  Hypothesise/Construct   ⎧Make ⎫
  ↓   or   ⎩Reflect⎭
  Test
  ↓
  Review

  Whatever model is adopted, however, it will probably conform to the following criteria,

  ● *It should encourage in students,*
    — *An openness to and respect for 'data'*
    — *A willingness to recognise and be prepared to modify their own perceptions*
    — *A commitment to learning how to learn.*
  ● *It will demand of teachers,*
    — *Provision of the means whereby students become more sophisticated writers and readers*
    — *A willingness to provide unambiguous structures for learning, and,*
    — *Skill in encouraging students to negotiate a departure from these structures in order to establish their own programmes of work.*

B. Students should be encouraged to relate theory and practice, to 'make' as well as to 'analyse'.

2.2. *Informing principles about the subject*
These principles are designed to suggest an approach to the subject capable of integrating work in Language, Literature and Communication. It is intended that the concepts should inform, sometimes implicitly, sometimes explicitly, the teacher's choice of and approach to the subject matter. They should not themselves form a programme of study.

A. Attention should be paid to the CONTEXT in which a text is produced (e.g. Historical, Social) and read (e.g. Psychological)

B. A preoccupation of this kind (in (A) above), which is wider than that traditionally associated with English Literature, can be achieved through Language Study.

   COMMENT:

   - *It can also be achieved through cross-curricular work – including interdisciplinary modules*
   - *The basis for developing an approach of this kind can be found in Raymond Williams' work on 'Key-words', in the JMB 'A' level English Language, and in a model of the language (ref. Douglas Barnes) that stresses 'MEANING and SIGNIFICANCE', 'FORMS and STRUCTURES' and 'SOCIAL CONTEXTS' in inter-action.*

C. In recognition that technological innovation has widened the range of 'texts' with which meaning is made and understood, to include, for example, Film and TV, the informing principles must include reference to semiotic as well as linguistic constructs.

2.3. *Content*

The content of the course should be expressed as an 'entitlement' curriculum:

A. Activities should include, for example,

   - The production of Film, TV and Still Photography
   - Talk ('enabling' and 'product')
   - Writing of a variety of kinds ('enabling' and 'product')
   - Analysis
   - Investigation

B. Exposure to a variety of 'texts' or 'representations' (these terms are used in order to suggest something other than an exclusive pre-occupation with books) including, for example,

   - Books (fiction and non-fiction)
   - Oral Language
   - Film/TV
   - Theatre
   - Non-literary forms of writing

2.4. *Introductory modules*

During the first term of the course, students would be required to complete 2 modules. (A) and (B) are options, (C) is required for all students. All three modules would be designed to integrate Language and Literature, Written and Spoken uses of the language, 'making' and 'analysing'. Whilst each module is equally concerned with 'text' and 'context', (A) and (B) start from the former, (C) from the latter.

A. Story-Telling

   COMMENT: To include, for example, work on the oral tradition, narrative, anecdote, telling stories etc.

B. Conversations

   COMMENT: To include, for example, analysis of small group talk, Diaries (conversations with oneself), letters, journals, playscripts, Telephone conversations, the relationship between gossip and literature.

C. Publishing

COMMENT: To include, for example, 'from drafts to print'. The contexts in which writers produce books ('Thomas Hardy and his readers'), editing, video (and radio/film) as publication, work on newspapers.

2.5. *Extension modules*

It is intended that the 'Extension' modules should be more specific, pursuing particular locally determined needs and interests. For this reason, they would be constructed by the School or College according to centrally prescribed criteria. A complete course would include the completion of 4 modules, one from each major category, each of which would amount to roughly one term's worth of study.

A. Categories

- Investigating Language
- Writing and Writers
- Reading and Readers
- Production (i.e. Film/TV/Theatre etc.)

B. Content

The extension modules would be required to cover work in a variety of the following genres (the list is provisional): Satire, Myth, Documentary, Popular Fiction, Comics, Diaries, Letters, Journalism, The Novel, Children's Lit., Poetry, Drama, Non-Fiction, 'the language of . . . (e.g. Institutions, Technology)'.

2.6. *Project module*

As a concluding element in the course, students would be required to undertake a sustained and extended piece of project or research work of their own. The topics would not be prescribed, and might be quite narrowly specific. The criteria about 'context' listed in 'Informing Principles about the subject', however, would remain relevant to the approval of project titles.

3. The model in practice

It would be necessary to establish a number of 'course determinants' to guide schools and colleges in devising courses. These might include, for example, the requirement that study should conform to the common core agreed between Exam boards for 'A' level syllabuses in 'English Literature', and/or that there should be a significant element of work designed to make connections across more than one medium. They would certainly establish more specific requirements about the nature and frequency of assessment procedures (e.g. End of module or end of course? Coursework or Case Study exam? etc. etc.) and include more detailed assessment objectives to guide the production of coursework.

In imagining how such a scheme might operate in practice, it is important to grasp something about the variety of different ways in which a modular course can be taught. The following 'charts' provide a number of examples, of relevance to all kinds of institutions, whatever their size.

Example 1 – Small Sixth Form: 1 'A' group, teaching shared between 2 teachers.

Term 1	Intro. Mod. A 'Story Telling'
	Intro. Mod. C 'Publishing'
2	Extension Mod. 'Writing and Writers'
3	Extension Mod. 'Investigating Language'
Term 4	Extension Mod. 'Reading and Readers'
5	Extension Mod. 'Production'
6	(Short half term) Project Mod.

This represents the most rigid application of modular thinking, and highlights many of the problems. Arguably the needs of the student have been sacrificed to the constraints of the course structure, so that work that might be more appropriate at an early stage is delayed simply because it is not covered until a later module. A course of this kind might also lack variety and be dogged by frequent assessment deadlines. A more flexible arrangement could overcome some of these difficulties,

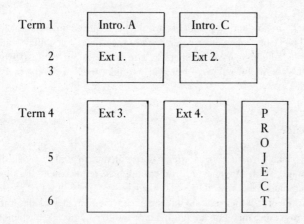

Example 2 – Sixth Form or Tertiary College: 6 'A' groups, 6 teachers.

In a small Sixth Form, the choice that characterises a modular curriculum is largely illusory for the student. Only the teacher actually experiences greater freedom to construct a course that he or she may consider more appropriate. Where a number of 'A' level groups run in parallel with each other, however, it is possible to provide options for the student. Timetabling would still represent a restraining influence, of course, and in this example it is imagined that only 3 groups are operating at the same time.

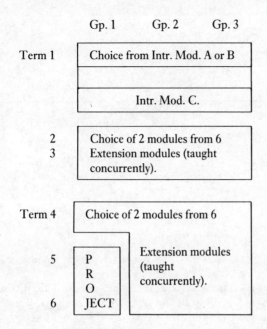

A system of this kind would require a more sophisticated system of personal tutoring than is normal since any single student might experience all 3 teachers in a variety of combinations. It might well be one requirement, however, that students be taught by the same teacher for their Introductory and Project Modules, and that this teacher act as an academic tutor.

4. Conclusion

It is important to bear in mind that the work above was completed in roughly 3 sessions at a conference and is by no means complete. We believe, however, that it represents a possible solution to the problems of curriculum fragmentation in Post 16 English.

Patrick Scott,
Barry Moorhouse,
Kevin Jeffery,
John Foggin,
George Keith.

Notes

1 Introduction

1 Sampson, A. (1982). *The Changing Anatomy of Britain.* London: Hodder and Stoughton.

2 Taken from Denys Thompson's address to the 1965 conference of NCTE on The aims and purposes of teaching English in Britain. Published in Squire, J. R. (ed.) (1966). *A Common Purpose.* Urbana, Ill.: NCTE.

3 As summarized by Greenwell, B. (1978). *Examinations at 18+ – The N & F Proposals and 'A' Level Developments.* NATE Examinations Booklet No. 2. Sheffield: NATE.

2 Literature I: custom . . .

1 HMI (1986). *A Survey of the Teaching of 'A' Level English Literature in 20 Mixed Sixth Forms in Comprehensive Schools.* London: DES.

2 JMB 'A' English Literature Paper II, alt. A, Q. 3a, June 1985.

3 JMB 'A' English Literature Paper II, alt. A, Q. 3b, June 1985.

4 JMB 'A' English Literature Paper II, alt. A, Q. 12b, June 1985.

5 ULSEB (1981). *GCE Examiner's Report – June 1981.* London: ULSEB.

6 AEB 'A' English Literature Paper 2, Q. 6b, November 1986.

7 JMB 'A' English Literature Paper I, Q. 3b, June 1985.

8 Leavis, F. R. (1952). Diabolic intellect and the noble hero. In *The Common Pursuit.* London: Chatto and Windus.

9 Carrington, N. T. (1976). *Brodie's Notes: Hardy, Tess of the D'Urbevilles.* Pan Study Aids. London: Pan.

10 AEB (1986). *Reports of Examiners.* Guildford: AEB.

11 JMB (1986). *GCE Examiners' Reports 1986: English.* Manchester: JMB.

12 AEB 'A' English Literature Paper 1, Q. 1, November 1986.

13 JMB 'A' English Literature Paper II, alt. A, Q. 5b, June 1985.

14 AEB 'A' English Literature Paper 1, Q. 8, November 1986.

15 AEB 'A' English Literature Paper 1, Q. 12, November 1986.

16 AEB 'A' English Literature Paper 1, Q. 6, November 1986.

17 JMB 'A' English Literature Paper I, Q. 6b, June 1985.

18 AEB 'A' English Literature Paper 2, Q. 1b, November 1986.

19 JMB 'A' English Literature Paper II, alt. A, Q. 2a, June 1985.

20 AEB 'A' English Literature Paper 1, Q. 4, November 1986.
21 AEB 'A' English Literature Paper 1, Q. 17, November 1986.

3 Literature II: . . . and practice
1 JMB 'A' English Literature Paper I, Q. 4b, June 1985.
2 AEB 'A' English Literature Paper 1, Q. 3, November 1986.

4 Literature III: the alternatives
1 The part played by the Cambridge Local Examinations Syndicate in developing open book examinations should also be acknowledged. The Cambridge GCE 'O' level 'plain texts' syllabus in English Literature was genuinely innovative.
2 AEB 'A' English Literature Alternative Syllabus Paper 2, Q. 3, June 1986.
3 AEB 'A' English Literature Alternative Syllabus Paper 2, Q. 26, June 1986.
4 AEB 'A' English Literature Alternative Syllabus Paper 2, Q. 30, June 1986.
5 AEB 'A' English Literature Alternative Syllabus Paper 2, Q. 21, June 1986.

5 Language I: language study or linguistics?
1 The quotation is from *Language in Use* (Doughty *et al.*, 1971). It should not be forgotten that *Language in Use* grew out of the Nuffield Programme in Linguistics and English Teaching (1964) directed by Professor M. A. K. Halliday.
2 Torbe, M. (1980). Language study in secondary education – some comments. *English in Education*, **14**(1).

6 Language II: which syllabus?
1 Unpublished minutes (circulated to all participants) of the Schools Council 16–19 Project Meeting on English at 'A' Level.
2 From *English (Language) at 'A' Level – Northern Joint Working Party: Draft Submission – Some General Comments* (March 1981). This was a commentary provided by the Schools Council 'A' level sub-committee for English at an 'interim stage before the submission reached its completed form'. The section from which the quotation is taken continues as follows: 'a greater degree of technical knowledge could legitimately be required, they thought, and this was most likely to be in "linguistics"'
3 June 1981.
4 Questions 1(a) and 2(a) are from the JMB 'A' English Language Paper 1, May 1986; questions 1(b) and 2(b) are from the ULSEB 'A' English Language Studies Paper 5, Specimen Paper 85/2, March 1985.
5 JMB 'A' English Language Paper 1, Q. 11, May 1986.
6 ULSEB 'A' English Paper 3, Q. 2, June 1981.
7 JMB (1986). *GCE Examiners' Reports 1986: English Language (Advanced)*. Manchester: JMB.

7 Language III: language and literature
1 All these rubrics are taken from ULSEB 'A' English Language Studies Specimen Paper 85/2, March 1985 (Specimen Papers A and B).

8 Communication I: 'A' level Communication Studies
1 AEB 'A' Communication Studies Paper 1, June 1985.
2 AEB 'A' Communication Studies Paper 1, June 1986.

3 Masterman, L. (1980). *Teaching about Television.* London: Macmillan.
4 Knight, R. (1984). The teaching about television debate – further discriminations. *English in Education*, **18**(3).
5 AEB 'A' Communication Studies Paper 1, Q. 3, June 1986.
6 AEB 'A' Communication Studies Paper 1, Q. 5, June 1986.
7 AEB 'A' Communication Studies Paper 1, Q. 4, June 1986.

9 Communication II: beyond Communication Studies
1 AEB 'A' Communication Studies Paper 1, Q. 3, June 1985.
2 AEB 'A' Communication Studies Paper 1, Q. 7, June 1986.
3 Beynon, J. *et al.* (1983). The politics of discrimination. *English in Education*, **17**(3).
4 Ibid.
5 Masterman, L. (1982). A response to Roger Knight. *English in Education*, **16**(3).

10 Conclusion
1 O'Connor, M. (1988). Fighting for breadth. *The Guardian*, 5 July.
2 Ibid.
3 HMI (1986). *A Survey of the Teaching of 'A' Level English Literature in 20 Mixed Sixth Forms in Comprehensive Schools.* London: DES.
4 The list of modules is taken from the Report of the CEE Communications Working Party of the SREB (June 1976).
5 Brief to the Higginson Committee.
6 Wragg, T. (1988). High time to take five. *The Guardian*, 14 June.
7 Proposed for AS level 'History, Literature and the Irish Identity 1890–1926', developed by the Institute of Irish Studies at the University of Liverpool.

Bibliography

Allen, D. (1980). *English Teaching since 1965: How Much Growth?*. London: Heinemann.

Associated Examining Board (1986). *Reports of Examiners*. Guildford: AEB.

Bennison, S. and Spicer, A. (1988). Challenging 'A' level. In *The English Magazine*. London: The ILEA English Centre.

Beynon, J., Doyle, B., Goulden, H. and Hartley, J. (1983). 'The politics of discrimination'. *English in Education*, **17**(3), 3–14.

Clarke, M. (1987). *Teaching Popular Television*. London: Heinemann.

Crystal, D. (1976). *Child Language, Learning and Linguistics*. London: Edward Arnold.

Department of Education and Science (1984). *English from 5 to 16*. London: HMSO.

Department of Education and Science (1986). *English from 5 to 16: The Responses*. London: HMSO.

Department of Education and Science (1988). *Report of the Committee of Inquiry into the Teaching of English Language*. London: HMSO.

Dixon, J. (1967). *Growth though English*. Oxford: Oxford University Press for NATE.

Dixon, J. (1979). *Education 16–19: The Role of English and Communications*. London: Macmillan.

Dixon, J. (1980). How to study language and the human mind. *English in Education*, **14**(3), 25–6.

Doughty, P., Pearce, J. and Thornton, G. (1971). *Language in Use*. London: Edward Arnold.

Doughty, P., Pearce, J. and Thornton, G. (1972). *Exploring Language*. London: Edward Arnold.

Eagleton, T. (1983). *Literary Theory: An Introduction*. Oxford: Blackwell.

Fairbairns, Z. (1979). *Benefits*. London: Virago.

Freeborn, D. (1982). Varieties of English. *The Times Educational Supplement*.

Graham, N. (1984). *Designing and Marking English Examinations: A Resource Booklet for Scarborough English Teachers*. Scarborough, Canada: Scarborough Board of Education.

Greenwell, B. (1988). *Alternatives at English 'A' Level*. Sheffield: NATE.

HMI (1986). *A Survey of the Teaching of 'A' Level English Literature in 20 Mixed Sixth Forms in Comprehensive Schools*. London: DES.

Joint Matriculation Board (1984). *GCE Examiners' Reports 1984: English*. Manchester: JMB.

Joint Matriculation Board (1986). *GCE Examiners' Reports 1986: English*. Manchester: JMB.

Jones, C. and Weller, M. (eds) (undated). *Personal Response*. Sheffield: NATE.

Knight, R. (1982). Understanding 'discrimination': the case against 'television studies'. *English in Education*, 16(3), 1–9.

Knight, R. (1984). The teaching about television debate: further discriminations. *English in Education*, 18(3), 50–61.

Limb, A. (ed.) (1986). *Language and Languages 16–19*. London: NCLE.

Marenbon, J. (1987). *English our English*. London: Centre for Policy Studies.

Masterman, L. (1980). *Teaching about Television*. London: Macmillan.

Masterman, L. (1982). A response to Roger Knight. *English in Education*, 16(3), 10–12.

Nay-Brock, P. (1987). *Who's Doing What? The Senior English Curriculum in Australian Schools*. Australia: AATE.

O'Connor, M. (1988). Fighting for breadth. *The Guardian*, 5 July.

Post-14 Committee (1988). *English 'A' Level in Practice*. Sheffield: NATE.

SSEC (1964). *The Examining of English Language*. London: HMSO.

Stork, F. C. (1980). Language study in secondary education. *English in Education*, 14(1), 23–9.

Torbe, M. (1980). Language study in secondary education – comments. *English in Education*, 14(1), 32–4.

University of London School Examinations Board (1981). *General Certificate of Education – Examiner's Report – June 1981*. London: ULSEB.

University of London School Examinations Board (1987). *Submission of Evidence to the Committee of Inquiry on the Teaching of English in Schools*. London: ULSEB.

Wallwork, J. F. (1969). *Language and Linguistics*. London: Heinemann.

Williams, R. (1977). *Marxism and Literature*. Oxford: Oxford University Press.

Williams, R. (1981). *Culture*. Glasgow: Fontana.

Williams, R. (1983). *Culture and Society 1780 – 1950*. Harmondsworth: Penguin.

Womack, P. (1987). Changing A-Levels. Unpublished.

Wragg, T. (1988). High time to take five. *The Guardian*, 14 June.

Index

Moorhouse, Barry, 135
multi-cultural education, 1, 6

National Association for Advisers in
    English (NAAE), 105, 130
National Association for the Teaching of
    English (NATE), 1, 35, 38, 42
National Congress on Languages in
    Education (NCLE), 103–4
National Council for the Teaching of
    English (NCTE), 10
Nay-Brock, Paul, 2
'new' sixth former, The, 12, 25
Northern Working Party on 'A' English
    Language, 50–2

Open University, The, 106
Owen, Wilfred, 58–61

Parry, John, 37
practical criticism, 3, 5, 6, 35, 59, 70,
    80–2
Schools Council, The, 12, 25, 65, 106
    English Committee, 50–2
    16–19 English Project, 103
Schools Examinations and Assessment
    Council (SEAC), 101
semiotics, 82, 88
skill shortages, 96–8
'specification (the process of)', 9–10

Southern Regional Examinations Board
    (SREB), 102
Spicer, Andrew, 89, 103
Standing Conference on University
    Entrance (SCUE), 12
Stockwell, Peter, 62
Stork, F. C., 46–7
study guides, 22–3

Teaching about Television (Len
    Masterman), 79, 81
Teaching Popular Television (Mike Clarke),
    81
Theatre Studies, 87–8
Thompson, Denys, 9
Times Educational Supplement, The, 57
Tom's Last Voyage (Peter Stockwell),
    62–4, 72, 109
Torbe, Mike, 47, 51

'Universal Truths', 9, 105

Wallwork, J. F., 57
Wessex Project, The, 101
Williams, Raymond, 8, 84–5, 90, 104,
    132
Womack, Peter, 8–10, 88
Wragg, Ted, 106

Youth Training Scheme, 98